T0360448

Literature and Leadership

Great literature provides didactic commentaries on universal themes in the drama of life and visceral lessons on leadership. The careful reading of timeless novels positions readers to emerge as astute protagonists in their own stories in the context of the grander narrative and internalize universal themes of the human story. Students of the great works of literature also emerge culturally literate, with a better understanding of themselves and others in relation to nobler virtues, traditions, and purposes. In addition to demonstrating great works of literature as among the first formal books on leadership, this book makes explicit connections between the study of literature and the research found in leadership and management studies.

This book:

- Provides a bridge between the robust literary world and the leadership and management genre.
- Demonstrates how language and literature uniquely develop leaders to have a sophisticated understanding of historical and contemporary cultures, events, and people.
- Documents how powerful narratives either promote or diminish human flourishing.
- Illustrates the usefulness of all great literature and stories in shaping engaging and compelling workplace narratives that inspire and engage the collective.
- Equips leaders and managers with the knowledge and skills to embrace the drama of leadership and engage in meaningful sensemaking to help organizations thrive.
- Encourages readers to be connoisseurs of great works of literature and include such works in their leadership libraries.

This book is ideal for the initiated and uninitiated in the study of literature and leadership by making explicit complementary and relevant insights to make reading and leading much more meaningful. Those unfamiliar with great literature will gain a deeper appreciation for books serving as tutors and mentors in the ways of leadership and become more discerning readers. Those unfamiliar with the leadership genre will improve their acumen to use endearing and enduring narratives to influence people and organizations.

John R. Shoup is Professor of Education, the Program Director for the PhD in Leadership Studies, and the Executive Director of the Dr. Paul and Annie Kienel Leadership Institute at California Baptist University in Riverside, California, US.

Troy W. Hinrichs is Professor of Criminal Justice and political science as well as a Fellow at the Dr. Paul and Annie Kienel Leadership Institute at California Baptist University in Riverside, California, US.

Leadership Horizons
Editors
John Shoup, California Baptist University, USA
Troy Hinrichs, California Baptist University, USA

The original and timeless research on leadership is situated in the classical works associated with the humanities. Great literature, art, theatre, philosophy, and music provide both existential and visceral insights to the drama of leadership beyond what traditional approaches to leadership studies have been able to furnish up to now. The classics in the humanities are didactic commentaries on universal themes associated with the challenges and hopes of good leadership. Knowledge of the classics provides a way of appreciating historical and contemporary cultures and a framework for thinking deeply about what is true, good, honorable, and beautiful. Returning the classics to the leadership genre equips leaders with a culturally informed language and narrative to develop the often ignored aesthetical aspects of leadership. This series connects lessons from various great works in art, literature, philosophy, theatre, and music to specific leadership research and contemporary leadership challenges. The series weaves the art and science of leadership studies and equips readers with multiple frames of reference to become aesthetically pleasing, engaging, and culturally astute leaders to make the right things happen the right way.

Leadership Horizons is relevant to students and researchers across business and management, organizational and institutional studies, and the humanities.

Books in the series:

Literature and Leadership
The Role of the Narrative in Organizational Sensemaking
John R. Shoup and Troy W. Hinrichs

Literature and Leadership

The Role of the Narrative in Organizational Sensemaking

**John R. Shoup and
Troy W. Hinrichs**

Routledge
Taylor & Francis Group

LONDON AND NEW YORK

First published 2020
by Routledge
2 Park Square, Milton Park, Abingdon, Oxon OX14 4RN

and by Routledge
52 Vanderbilt Avenue, New York, NY 10017

Routledge is an imprint of the Taylor & Francis Group, an informa business

British Library Cataloguing-in-Publication Data
A catalogue record for this book is available from the British Library

Library of Congress Cataloging-in-Publication Data
Names: Shoup, John R., author. | Hinrichs, Troy W., author.
Title: Literature and leadership: the role of the narrative in
organizational sensemaking / John R. Shoup and Troy W. Hinrichs.
Description: Abingdon, Oxon ; New York, NY: Routledge, 2020. |
Series: Leadership horizons |
Includes bibliographical references and index.
Identifiers: LCCN 2019017381 | ISBN 9780367266455 (hardback) |
ISBN 9780429294365 (ebook)
Subjects: LCSH: Leadership. | Leadership in literature. |
Literature and society. | Organizational sociology.
Classification: LCC HM1261 .S56135 2020 | DDC 302.3/5—dc23
LC record available at https://lccn.loc.gov/2019017381

ISBN: 978-0-367-26645-5 (hbk)
ISBN: 978-0-429-29436-5 (ebk)

Typeset in Baskerville
by codeMantra

To Margarita Shoup, You adorn my soul and bring the *joie de vivre* to our story. – John

To Paige Hinrichs, You are the heroine in our love story and the seal over my heart. – Troy

To Steve and Barbara Cockerham, Your well-read and well-lived lives are a story that all should know. Thank you for your legacy.

Contents

Preface

A handwritten manuscript found in Harry Truman's desk after his death made explicit what many great leaders have long recognized. Truman noted that "readers of good books, particularly books of biography and history, are preparing themselves for leadership." He went on to state that "not all readers become leaders. But all leaders must be readers."[1]

This book echoes Truman's conviction and establishes that leaders and managers should be connoisseurs of great literature if they wish to have endearing and enduring impacts on their personal and professional communities. He was convinced that the insights from the great authors provided the meta-narratives for leaders and managers to better fulfill their sensemaking responsibilities, the core duty that defines their roles. Whether they realize it or not, leaders shape and manage their organizational narratives. Stories abound in the workplace, especially around what the leaders do and say or don't do and say. People need to make sense of their lives, especially their fit and worth in the workplace. Far better that people adopt well-crafted organizational narratives from their leaders than default to self-serving stories in the form of gossip and other toxic or misinformed narratives. This book demonstrates that great literature is a primary source for leaders and managers to shape expectations around more meaningful, empathetic, and direction giving narratives.

Leaders are sensemakers. The use of compelling narratives in the work environment makes much sense, given the fact that people are *homo narrans* – storytelling people. Fisher (1987) posited that "all forms of communication need to be seen fundamentally as stories – symbolic interpretations of aspects of the world occurring in time and shaped by history, culture, and character" (p. xi). Philosopher and linguist Umberto Eco (1983) asserted that humans are storytelling animals by nature (p. 13). Storytelling is the preferred means of engaging and entertaining one another. Stories are ubiquitous, even in art, film, and music. Lucaites and Condit (1985) argued that storytelling "represents a universal medium of consciousness"

(p. 90). Muehlhoff and Langer (2017) were very explicit in their assertion that "we think in stories" (p. 115). The best way to develop and communicate endearing and enduring stories is by mirroring what is found in great literature.

Leaders are storytellers. The question remains: what type of stories are they using to communicate core values, inspire colleagues, and promote engagement? This is where great literature, especially novels, become primary sources for leaders to discern and implement virtuous and meaningful sensemaking stories that transcend people, time, and place. This book is a clarion call for leaders and managers to return to great books for tutelage and mentoring in the science and art of sensemaking (i.e., leading).

Despite the benefits of a good narrative in understanding and connecting with people emotionally, most business leaders and managers have been reluctant, if not remiss, to include the classics and storytelling in their leadership practices (Hutchinson, 2018; Forman, 2013). Fryer (2003) noted that "most executives struggle to communicate, let alone inspire. Too often, they get lost in the accoutrements of company speak: PowerPoint slides, dry memos, and hyperbolic missives from the corporate communications department" (p. 51). Additionally, leaders and managers are too "busy, harried, quick to calculate the dollar value of their time, bombarded by multiple messages from a dizzying number of communication channels, and likely to respond in haste and in kind to what comes their way" to take time for stories (Forman, 2013, p. 3). The tide is shifting a bit as many organizations are recognizing that making meaning is critical to making money and that stories have sensemaking capabilities to simplify the busyness, focus practices, and get stakeholders on the same page, beyond what can be accomplished by multiple memos, messages, and training manuals.

This book is part of the *Leadership Horizon* series that reintroduces art, literature, theatre, music, and philosophy into the leadership studies genre. Great works of fiction serve as didactic commentaries on universal themes in the drama of life, providing more visceral lessons than more traditional leadership and management books are able to offer. The careful reading of timeless novels enables readers to emerge as astute protagonists in their own story in the context of a grander narrative while internalizing universal themes of the human story. Students of great literature enhance their cultural literacy and increase their emotional intelligence with a better understanding of themselves and others in relation to nobler virtues, traditions, and purposes. In addition to demonstrating the utility of great novels as being among the first formal books on leadership, this book makes explicit connections between the study of literature and the research found in leadership and management studies.

This book builds a bridge between the robust literary world and the leadership and management genre, demonstrating how language and literature uniquely develops leaders. Novels are both mirrors and windows to a more sophisticated understanding of historical and contemporary cultures, events, people, and life. They also provide exemplars for people to craft inspiring and engaging personal and professional workplace narratives. Put simply, great literature provides people with a good sense of plot, purpose, and performance for their storytelling. This book demonstrates that leaders are readers and storytellers, and, as such, should include great novels in their leadership libraries.

The first chapter of this book explores the impact of great literature on the culture broadly and readers specifically. It documents how great literature captures and shapes culture, and serves as a primary resource that civilizations use to develop and promote identity around cherished values and virtues. The chapter also describes what works of great literature have in common regarding themes, plot, and characterization, and illustrates how words and story refine people's beliefs, dispositions, and habits. Leaders will be inspired and equipped to be connoisseurs of great literature and cultivate enlightened perspectives on life in general and leadership specifically.

It should be noted that the authors are not necessarily engaging in the larger debate as to what is or is not canon. Although there are a relative handful of works of fiction that are nearly universally upheld as classics or "great," those terms can be loaded with all manner of political or social import. Indeed, novels are a relatively recent art form compared to painting, sculpture, and music. Individual novels often have a temporary impact. Writing about novels of early 19th-century America, Nina Baym (1984) noted, "Since some notion of permanence has always attached to the idea of great art, this transitoriness intensified the difficulty of defining the 'better novel' within the popular framework" (pp. 48–49). This volume will use three novels that are widely considered great for a variety of reasons, not least of which is that they have "stood the test of time."

The second chapter discusses in some depth the three novels chosen as examples for connecting great literature with leadership and management: *Don Quixote*, *Pride and Prejudice*, and *Moby-Dick*. It uses these famous works of Cervantes, Austen, and Melville to illustrate the features of great literature addressed in Chapter 1 and provides context for the explicit connections to good leadership developed in Chapter 3. Chapter 2 also provides a brief book report-like description of each novel's historical context, a brief biography of each author, and a synopsis of the respective plots and main themes as a prelude to Chapter 3.

Chapter 3 elaborates and expands on themes from each novel and connects them to contemporary leadership research and practices. The chapter demonstrates how great novels portray with elevated language and perspectives the universal themes and characters that leaders and managers encounter and handle in the workplace. The chapter illuminates how the great stories are mirrors and windows for leaders and managers to groom their leadership practices by providing timeless lessons from engaging plots. Such lessons include the role of storytelling and sensemaking in optimizing the work of the collective and the consequences of quixotic (Don Quixote), obsessive (Ahab), and haughty (Mr. Darcy) acts of leadership.

The final chapter explores how leaders acting as storytellers (i.e., sensemakers) have transformed and developed high-performing organizational work cultures. This chapter illustrates that people rally around compelling stories to embrace organizational visions and missions, streamline work priorities, and legitimize loyalty to their respective groups. It concludes with principles and tactics for leaders to craft and communicate endearing stories that will help their organizations thrive, demonstrating the value of good narratives highlighted in the previous chapters.

This book is ideal for both the initiated and uninitiated in the study of literature and leadership. Those unfamiliar with great literature will gain a deeper appreciation for novels as tutors and mentors in the ways of leadership and become more discerning readers. Those unfamiliar with the leadership genre will improve their acumen to use endearing and enduring narratives to influence people and organizations. Those already astute in good literature and/or leadership studies will deepen their understanding of leaders as sensemakers on par with authors of great literature. Regardless, whether one is a novice or an expert, the four chapters work in concert to provide all readers complementary and relevant insights that will make reading and leading much more enjoyable, meaningful, and impactful.

Happy reading and leading!

Note

1 Post-Presidential Papers. Truman went on to note that "Many readers become historians and teachers. They are retiring, timid when publicity is involved, and are among the greatest assets to this republic."

References

Baym, N. (1984). *Novel readers and novel reading.* Ithaca, NY: Cornell University Press.

Eco, U. (1983). *The name of the rose.* San Diego, CA: Harcourt Brace Jovanovich.

Fisher, W. R. (1987). *Human communication as narration: Toward a philosophy of reason, value, and action.* Columbia, SC: University of South Carolina Press.

Forman, J. (2013). *Storytelling in business: The authentic and fluent organization.* Palo Alto, CA: Stanford University Press.

Fryer, B. (2003). Storytelling that moves people. *Harvard Business Review, 81,* 51–55.

Hutchinson, K. (2018). *Leadership and small business: The power of stories.* Cham, Switzerland: Springer Nature.

Lucaites, J. L., & Condit, C. M. (1985). Re-constructing narrative theory: A functional perspective. *Journal of Communication, 35*(4), 90–108. doi:10.1111/j.1460-2466.1985.tb02975.x

Muehlhoff, T. & Langer, R. (2017). *Winsome persuasion: Christian influence in a post-Christian world.* Downers Grove, IL: IVP Academic, an imprint of InterVarsity Press.

Acknowledgments

Thank you Gisel Mendez, Kylie Venezia, and Melanie Thomas for serving as our graduate assistants and formatting the final manuscript.

About the authors

John R. Shoup is a Professor of Education, the Program Director for the PhD in Leadership Studies, and the Director of the Dr. Paul and Annie Kienel Leadership Institute at California Baptist University in Riverside, California. He teaches leadership and educational history and policy at the graduate level and has conducted research and workshops on leadership development and best practices. He also served as a school principal, university dean, and has worked in various social service settings. John is an author and frequent presenter on topics related to leadership. He has a PhD in Education with an emphasis in Educational Administration and Policy Studies from the University of California, Riverside. He also has a Master of Divinity and a Master of Arts in Counseling Psychology from Trinity Evangelical Divinity School in Deerfield, IL. He has been married for 30 years to Margarita and has one daughter, Rebecca.

Troy W. Hinrichs is a Professor of Criminal Justice and political science as well as a Fellow at the Dr. Paul and Annie Kienel Leadership Institute at California Baptist University in Riverside, California. He teaches Criminal Law, Legal Reasoning, and International Law at the graduate level as well as Constitutional Law, Criminal Law, Law and Literature, and Humanities at the undergraduate level. He has conducted research and presented on leadership and literature as well as on the Insanity Defense and religious liberty. He has also worked as an attorney at the Texas Department of Public Safety and has taught at various colleges and universities in Texas and California, including International Law in California State University San Bernardino's MA in National Security Studies program since 2006. Troy earned his Juris Doctorate from the Texas Tech University School of Law in Lubbock, TX. He also has degrees in English and Philosophy from Hardin-Simmons University in Abilene, TX. He has been married for over 22 years to Paige and has two sons, Joshua and Zachary, and one daughter, Sabrina.

1 Reading the good and the good from reading

Great literature both captures and shapes culture and people. It is a primary resource that societies use to anchor their identity around celebrated ideals, values, and virtues. This chapter explores the question "What is good literature?" It illustrates what good novels have in common and how the power of words and story refine and develop one's beliefs, dispositions, and habits. The chapter inspires and equips readers to be connoisseurs of good literature so as to become aesthetically aware, culturally astute, and principled leaders.

Finding the good

Not all stories are created equally. The 19th-century German philosopher Arthur Schopenhauer noted in his essay *On Reading and Books* (Schopenhauer, 1851/1882):

> Hence, in regard to our subject, the art of *not* reading is highly important. This consists in not taking a book into one's hand merely because it is interesting to the great public at the time — such as political or religious pamphlets, novels, poetry, and the like, which make a noise and reach perhaps several editions in their first and last years of existence. Remember rather that the man who writes for fools always finds a large public: and only read for a limited and definite time exclusively the works of great minds, those who surpass other men of all times and countries, and whom the voice of fame points to as such. These alone really educate and instruct. One can never read too little of bad, or too much of good books: bad books are intellectual poison; they destroy the mind. In order to read what is good, one must make it a condition never to read what is bad; for life is short, and both time and strength limited.

Not everyone agrees that there are universal standards of greatness in art or literature. Literary critic Nicholas Shakespeare (2016) noted in the *Daily Telegraph* in a review of a book on 20th-century British literary culture that,

> 'Taste' has fewer guides. There is no single mainstream. The influence once exerted by a circle of middle-class male Londoners has dissolved into the Amazon free-for-all, where every reader is a critic, even if they can find it problematic to distinguish a novel from a biography or, in extreme cases, a book from a beanbag.

While taste is not just difficult to measure but surely impossible to quantify, a common measure is the so-called "test of time." Hipple (1992) wrote:

> It is commonplace in literary studies to suggest that one of the standards by which classic literature is so identified is that the novel or play or poem has "stood the test of time." In essence, this criterion holds that a work cannot be a classic unless and until it has been read by generations of readers beyond the time of its writing. Thus, Twain's *Adventures of Huckleberry Finn* easily makes the list, as does most of Dickens and Hardy and Jane Austen and virtually all of Shakespeare. Curiously, a book does not necessarily have to be read in its own time – just in succeeding times; witness *Moby Dick*, not a popular novel when Melville first published it but eminently so after its first few decades of sparse readership.
>
> (p. 5)

The "test of time" standard goes beyond mere faddishness. Novels that may be considered great or important or even just popular may not be read at all by subsequent generations. J.K. Rowling's *Harry Potter* series, as but one example, may or may not be seen on a par with J.R.R. Tolkien's *The Lord of the Rings* trilogy or C.S. Lewis's *Chronicles of Narnia* series in another 40 years. Rowling's books may surpass those in reputation. That is not to say one series of books is better than or worse than the others. The test of time is a reasonable measure of long-term appreciation and quality but not a foolproof test of "greatness" or substantiveness or depth. Indeed, many great novels undoubtedly get left behind as time marches on, authors die, tastes change and older books get lost in the glut of newer books in the current publishing boom. Author and professor C.S. Lewis (1944/1970) advocated the reading of "old books" noting that people of any generation suffer a sort of blindness from being surrounded only by current ideas and philosophies and largely ignorant, or hostile to, past or future ideas and assumptions. He wrote:

> None of us can fully escape this blindness, but we shall certainly increase it and weaken our guard against it, if we only read modern

books. Where they are true they will give us truths which we half knew already. Where they are false they will aggravate the error with which we are already dangerously ill. The only palliative is to keep the clean sea breeze of the centuries blowing through our minds, and this can only be done by reading old books.

(p. 202)

Lewis (1944/1970) went on to note that while mere age doesn't imbue books with special wisdom, reading old books can help us avoid contemporary mistakes. In other words, reading about past cultures and characters can inform us of our current times and potential troubles that lie ahead. As Lewis wrote,

People were no cleverer then than they are now; they made as many mistakes as we. But not the *same* mistakes. . . . Two heads are better than one, not because either is infallible, but because they are unlikely to go wrong in the same direction.

(p. 202)

While, to some degree "beauty is in the eye of the beholder" (or reader in this case), most scholars and teachers would agree that some books are better for us than others even if there is not universal consensus on which specific books would be better. These good books are not akin to the Brussel sprouts (or insert detested vegetable here) of childhood, that while "good for us" are not enjoyable. On the other end of the spectrum, some books are so light and fluffy, they are akin to junk food – delicious, but empty and loaded with unfulfilling calories. These books are enjoyable for a fleeting moment, but if over-consumed can lead to longer term negative consequences – lazy thinking and bad ideas among others. Which books are good and which are bad? This volume will not purport to fully answer that question. Instead, this chapter will provide some guidance as to what books are beneficial and to argue that, unlike Brussel sprouts, these "good for you" books are not just healthy mentally, emotionally, and spiritually – but are also enjoyable – like a good steak. In other words, people can have their steak and read it too.

Good quality

The quality and quantity of reading are related issues. Author and professor Karen Swallow Prior (2018) noted that merely reading widely is insufficient to garner the benefits of reading books. She expanded on the theme that people must read not just for quantity but also for quality. "One must read virtuously," she stated (p. 14). Reading good books takes some effort. Rarely is the worthwhile thing easy. Reading books that demand the reader's thought and time is akin to exercise. The more one works out that "reading muscle," the easier and more rewarding reading becomes. Learning to enjoy the complexity and universality of great books is a major part of the journey. This vicarious experiencing of complex and universal settings and characteristics equips the reader to properly and adequately handle the often tangled knot of real-life problems and personalities. On the other end of the spectrum, Noel Carroll (1994) wrote of "junk fiction" that:

> Indeed, their story dimension is the most important thing about them. Stephen King, for instance, makes this point by saying that he is primarily a story teller, rather than a writer. Junk fictions aspire to be page-turners – the blurb on the cover of *Stillwatch* by Mary Higgins Clark says that it is "designed to be read at breathtaking speed" – and what motivates turning the page so quickly is our interest in what happens next. We do not dawdle over Clark's diction as we might over Updike's nor do we savor the complexity of her sentence structure, as we do with Virginia Woolf's. Rather, we read for story.
>
> Moreover, junk fictions are the sort of narratives that commentators are wont to call formulaic. That is, junk fictions generally belong to well-entrenched genres, which themselves are typified by their possession of an extremely limited repertoire of story-types.
>
> (pp. 225–226)

Leaving aside Carroll's characterization of many mass market novels as "junk" fiction, his point remains that some novels aim for more complex story and characterization by using more complex sentence and style and avoiding standard tropes of character and plot. Needless to say, many great works also trade in archetypal figures and plots such as the quest, the redemption story, and the Christ figure to name but a few.

What makes a novel great?

The questions of what makes literature great, how to identify great literature, and how to apply the benefits that flow from reading great literature, can be daunting, especially to the uninitiated. This and the following chapter also explore what great novels have in common despite their different settings, characters, and plots. Broadly speaking, great novels, those that stand "the test of time" or reach some level of universal acclaim, will often (though not solely – there are always exceptions to general rules) touch on universal themes, characters and plots, setting and symbolism that transcend culture and time (Baym, 1979).

Common elements of good literature (i.e., good story)

Plot

There is some debate as to how many basic plots there are and that debate is beyond the scope of this chapter, but the various lists have some commonalities: quests (of which *Don Quixote* and *Moby-Dick* have aspects), overcoming adversity, comedy (of which *Don Quixote* and *Pride and Prejudice* have aspects), tragedy, and others.[1] Taking the three novels discussed herein as exemplars of good and great novels: each of the novels present some aspects of many of the fundamental plots. *Don Quixote* has elements of a quest as well as comedy as readers follow Don Quixote and his squire Sancho Panza on their series of misadventures seeking fame and fortune. Cervantes also uses his novel to satirize and critique Spanish mores and society. Likewise, *Moby-Dick* contains multiple plot aspects including the quest plot as Ahab and his crew relentlessly pursue the titular white whale. It also has aspects of tragedy as the captain and crew lose everything as a result of arrogance among other character traits that contribute to the demise of the crew of the *Pequod*. Likewise, *Pride and Prejudice* has aspects of different core plots. It is considered by many to be a comedy. Jane Austen occasionally, but gently, pointedly satirizes the social structure of Great Britain as well as the social mores regarding marriage, the landed gentry and the ways that the different strata of society can suffer from pride and prejudice. Austen expertly guides us to the story's conclusion by setting up and then resolving the conflict that initially separates the protagonists and then ultimately brings them closer together. The ability to incorporate various plot devices expertly is one way to identify great literature. The great authors provide compelling stories in ways that avoid contrivance, but − even if set in an extraordinary or exotic locale or era − strike the reader as familiar − even universal.

Character

Great novels have at least one great protagonist − a main character that drives the plot and is the hero or at least the one whom the reader "roots for." Many novels have multiple protagonists or a rich array of characters that populate the novel and provide various opportunities to highlight and represent values and traits. Great novels also have an (or multiple) antagonist − a main character (or whale perhaps) who challenges the protagonist along the way to the novel's conclusion. There is no formula for what constitutes a good protagonist or antagonist, but the ones in the three examples used in this book are emblematic. Great characters, like great novels, often stand the test of time and usually have one or more character traits that help the audience empathize with their struggles and successes. Great antagonists are also often characters with whom the audience initially identifies. They are sometimes the more interesting of the two main characters.

One of the more famous examples is the general conclusion that in John Milton's epic *Paradise Lost,* the character of Satan is much more complex and interesting than his portrayal of God. That's not too surprising given the limits in portraying God as anything other than as perfect given Milton's censorious time. Villains are often more liberating for an author in terms of portraying character. *Moby-Dick* is a good example. Ishmael, the narrator and protagonist of the novel is a good-natured sort and somewhat of an innocent. He's an interesting character and one with whom we empathize and identify. But Captain Ahab, the antagonist, is the "juicier" character with all of his obsessive rage and mysterious habits. He is, in almost every way, more extreme than Ishmael and Melville highlights Ahab's lack of virtues in ways that Ishmael never could. In *Pride and Prejudice,* Jane Austen does not use a main antagonist though there are a few characters who work to keep the two protagonists apart. Austen mostly makes Elizabeth Bennet and Mr. Darcy, the two protagonists, their own worst enemies. It is their character flaws that work to frustrate their own desires and thus she is able to use their growth in emotional intelligence and self-discovery to resolve the main conflict of the novel. Austen simultaneously fills their world with interesting minor characters who exemplify and satirize various aspects of English society.

Character development through depiction and not solely through explicit description is also an aspect of great novels and characterization. For example, Elizabeth Bennet, the female protagonist in *Pride and Prejudice*, is portrayed as prejudiced toward Mr. Darcy, the main male protagonist, and others of the upper classes of British society. Of course, Austen sometimes explicitly describes Elizabeth as prideful, prejudiced, or joyful, but the more impactful illustrations of her come through plot, or from another character's description of her or in the moments of self-discovery expressed in conversation or the written letters between various characters. In describing the depth of her marital bliss compared to her sister Jane's own successful marriage she writes in a letter to her aunt that "I am happier even than Jane; she only smiles, I laugh." (Austen, 1813/2003, p. 369) Great authors can often say much with relative clarity enhanced by brevity. A skill with language is an obvious hallmark of great novels. It also illustrates good novels can inspire and equip people generally, and leaders specifically, to become experienced connoisseurs of good literature in a quest to cultivate and promote self-discovery, emotional intelligence, and ultimately effective and empathetic leadership.

Reading fiction is good; reading well is better

Great narrative fiction can help readers identify and learn to overcome internal and external challenges. G.K. Chesterton (1909/2009) posited:

> Fairy tales, then, are not responsible for producing in children fear, or any of the shapes of fear; fairy tales do not give the child the idea of the evil or the ugly; that is in the child already, because it is in the world already. Fairy tales do not give the child his first idea of bogey. What fairy tales give the child is his first clear idea of the possible defeat of bogey. The baby has known the dragon intimately ever since he had an imagination. What the fairy tale provides for him is a St. George to kill the dragon.
>
> (p. 130)

It is almost cliché to say that reading books is good for people. Parents, teachers, publishers, librarians, et al. say it often and most, if not all, people take it as a true statement. But the axiom begs to be explored further. Why are books good for people? If, as stated, books are "good" for people what does "good" mean? Healthy? Educational? Spiritually edifying? As an escape from the good and bad stressors of life? Are all books good? Some books? If only some, then which books are better? What kind of books? Non-fiction; fiction, or technical or some of each? It stands to reason, then, that if books are good for everyone, then reading books, and specifically reading "good books," would be especially important for leaders in all areas of human endeavor.

While the novel is a relatively modern medium for storytelling in the West, Greek philosopher Aristotle wrote about the importance of storytelling, plot, and character during the 4th century BCE.[2] In his work *Poetics*, Aristotle, discussing poetry and drama (akin to the coming discussion on novels, though drama and poetry will be dealt with more specifically in future volumes of this series), called fictional works "imitations" (Aristotle, trans. 1996). Malcolm Heath (1996) noted that "Aristotle's conception of poetry as imitation is therefore consistent with (though not identical to) that of fiction" (p. xiv). "Imitation" does not literally mean a direct copy of actual people or situations. Aristotle argued,

> It is clear from what has been said that the function of the poet is not to say what *has* happened, but to say the kind of thing that *would* happen, i.e. what is possible in accordance with probability or necessity.
>
> (Aristotle, trans. 1996, 9)

He also observed that poets tend to refer to universal truths and characteristic to plot and character as opposed to history's (non-fiction) penchant for dealing with particulars, i.e. actual people and actual times (Aristotle, 9; 51b).

Reading narrative fiction, novels in this discussion, permits the reader to experience and explore possibilities that might not actually occur, but could possibly occur. It also allows readers to experience and explore other cultures, ideas, eras and characters which mimic broadly, if not exactly, real-life experiences. Good fiction generally highlights and explores universal truths and traits even if the specific cultural settings are different from our own. This allows readers to identify and empathize with others across cultural divides and from different eras.

In 1344 AD, approximately a century before the invention of the Gutenberg printing press, an English bishop named Richard de Bury (1344/2006) wrote a short book entitled *The Philobiblon*. The book's title is literally "the love of books" in Greek, though the book was written in Latin as was the practice at the time of its writing. "Known as an inveterate book lover, de Bury spent much of his estate (and perhaps more) purchasing a rather large library – an especially luxurious pursuit given that all books were written by hand" before Gutenberg's printing press.[3] He wrote his rather short volume to celebrate the importance of books as well as the virtue of not just reading books, but the loving of books. As Matthew Battles noted in an Introduction to *The Philobiblon*, "Book are friends and ambassadors, guides and pathfinders, teachers and counselors. They abolish time and distance – powers easily purchased in our time, which were dearer by far in the late Middle Ages." (Battles, 2006, p. x). Given the proliferation of books today, de Bury's view that the "treasure of wisdom" is in all books is most likely overstated (in light of the comparative lack of books in his day). The general idea – that wisdom is contained in books and thus books are important – not just as technical manuals or data sources, but as resources for how to live life well, is still relevant.

De Bury recommending that leaders, especially, should be lovers of books, wrote:

> It is plain and evident who ought to be the chief lover of books. For those who have most need of wisdom in order to perform usefully the duties of their position, they are without doubt the most especially bound to show more abundantly to the sacred vessels of wisdom the anxious affection of a grateful heart.
>
> (de Bury, 1344/2006, p. 51)

He continued the argument, writing that "Wherefore princes and prelates, judges and doctors, and all other leaders of the commonwealth, as more than others they have need of wisdom, so more than others ought they to show zeal for the vessels of wisdom [books]" (de Bury, 1344/2006, p. 51). He also noted that leaders cannot properly lead without books. Even pre-Renaissance, it was recognized that proper leadership required knowledge and wisdom and that reading and reading well provided one of the best, if not the best, avenues to those qualities. The technological limitations of de Bury's era made discerning between "good" and "bad" books easier. Assuming that classics and those works considered worthy by a consensus of those in a position to order and pay transcribers to hand-written copies of pre-existing works, limited the production of original works and thus limited the debate – if for no other reason than it limited choices. Questions of quality have always existed, but the debate was inherently limited by the technological limitations and the resulting dearth of books that existed before the age of the printing press.

Good entertainment

In addition to providing guidance in wisdom, reading books, novels particularly, serves the twin purposes of making learning more enjoyable (or at the very least more palatable) and making life in general more pleasurable. Very few people learn from harangues or sermons – at least not most of the time. Great novels can illustrate lessons in courage or cowardice, honesty or dishonesty, generosity or stinginess in an entertaining way. For many, a well-told story can supplement or replace even the most noble or well-meaning lecture on good behavior by a teacher, parent, or trainer. Novelists portray these human traits undergoing various stressors in the plot allowing the reader to live vicariously while observing how the various characters experience and react to those same events.

Great stories offer more than mere entertainment to their readers and listeners. As Chesterton noted earlier about fairytales and dragons, stories carry information and lessons beyond the basic narrative, characterizations, and plot. Cultures are shaped and transmitted through great stories, books, songs, poems, and art. Stories especially are vehicles for sharing ideals thus transforming society and individuals. Books, especially narrative fiction (novels, shorts stories, novellas, et al.), have an important role in communicating culture and shaping ideas, values, knowledge and in entertaining readers. Novels can transport readers to long ago times, faraway places, and to cultures foreign and otherwise unknown. They allow readers to go places and experience circumstances they might otherwise never encounter. People live, in many ways, in a golden age of novels. Modern conveniences like e-readers, smartphone apps, and audio books allow people unparalleled access to literature. People even 20 years ago would marvel at the array of choices in literature – fiction, non-fiction, and technical – that we have today. While the "brick and mortar" bookstores of the previous centuries are slowly disappearing, online retailers have exploded to provide a dizzying array of choices. Besides issues of intellectual property and the debate over ownership of "actual" books versus owning digital downloads or audio recordings of books, this unprecedented access raises anew the evergreen issue of "what to read."

Good books help build good character

Additionally, as Prior (2018) noted, "Plot reveals character. And the act of judging the traits of a character shapes the reader's own character" (p. 20). Great authors populate their works with positive and negative characters for the reader to either emulate or to act as deterrents. This "lesson" is less obvious since it is embedded in a great story, description or characterization and not a lecture or sermon. Nussbaum (1995), in her book *Poetic Justice*, stated that reading "provides insights that should play a role . . . in the construction of an adequate moral and political theory . . ." (p. 12). She also noted that novel-reading helps readers develop "moral capacities" needed to turn those theories into a reality in public life. Novel-reading is not a silver bullet for societal and political ills but can play a major part in the moral development of leaders and followers (p. 12). Reading novels is also not a panacea for a lack of virtue, of course, but it can provide trenchant examples for those willing to learn. Nussbaum writing about Charles Dickens's novel *Hard Times* stated:

> This novel tells a story. In so doing, it gets its readers involved with the characters, caring about their projects, their hopes and fears participating in their attempts to unravel the mysteries and perplexities of their lives. The participation of the reader is made explicit at many points in the narration. And it is brought home to readers that the story is in certain ways their own story, showing possibilities for human life and choice that are in certain respects their own to seize, though their concrete circumstances may differ greatly.
>
> (p. 31)

Nussbaum (1995) highlighted a similar concept dealt with by Scottish philosopher and economist Adam Smith. Smith, in his work *The Theory of Moral Sentiments*, highlighted an idea which Nussbaum called the "judicious spectator" (p. 72). The judicious spectator is able to judge circumstances from a proper distance – not so close as to be prejudiced but also not so remote as to be utterly unfeeling. Indeed, Smith invoked human imagination as one way people experience and learn proper moral responses to their fellow humans. Smith (1759/1976) observed:

> As we have no immediate experience of what other men feel, we can form no idea of the manner in which they are affected, but by conceiving what we ourselves should feel in the like situation. Though our brother is upon the rack, as long as we ourselves are at our ease, our senses will never inform us of what he suffers. They never did, and never can, carry us beyond our own person, and it is by the imagination only that we can form any conception of what are his sensations. By the imagination we place ourselves in his situation, we conceive ourselves enduring all the same torments, we enter as it were into his body, and become in some measure the same person . . .
>
> (p. 9)

According to Griswold (2006), Smith also noted that this detachment not only gives the reader, or spectator, insight into the character and his or her response to a given situation but also provides a measure of objectivity. Smith argued that when readers sympathize with a fictional character's joys and pains, the process is akin to those same readers sympathizing with real people in everyday life (Griswold, 2006). Reading narrative fiction, especially novels, can give readers experience in building empathy and sympathy for trials and tribulations that are both outside their normal experience and universal to all humankind. The regular reading of well-written plots and characters hones a proper emotional and moral response – much like training. Of course, the imagination is not a perfect bridge and is not an exact replica of true "real-world" emotions, morals, and problems. In addition, there may well be well-written and characterized books with morally negative messages, so novels are not a foolproof guide to proper moral responses (Nussbaum, 1995).

Empirical Evidence of Goodness

Anecdotal and philosophical arguments are not the only evidence in favor of reading – and reading well. A growing body of empirical research is attempting to measure the value of reading literary fiction. Chapter 3 describes the Don Quixote effect – exposure to good stories nudges people toward more altruistic behavior, just as reading chivalric novels was the impetus for Don Quixote to become a knight-errant. In a study comparing the relative benefit to those who read a lot of fiction ("bookworms" in the parlance of the researchers) and those who read mostly non-fiction ("nerds" as the researchers labeled this cohort) Mar, Oatley, Hirsh, de la Paz, and Peterson (2006) noted:

> Stories contain depictions of the actual world replete with intentional agents pursuing goals to form a plot, whereas expository texts, in contrast, share no such parallels with the actual world. The processing of narratives, then, shares some similarities with the processing of our real social environment. Thus, frequent readers of narrative fiction, individuals who could be considered 'bookworms,' may bolster or maintain social-processing skills whilst reading stories, although they are removed from actual social contact during this activity. Conversely, frequent readers of nonfiction expository texts, individuals colloquially referred to as 'nerds,' could be headed toward an embodiment of the socially awkward stereotype by removing themselves from the actual social realm while not simulating experience in a fictional one. There exists both theoretical and empirical support for this hypothesis.
>
> (p. 695)

The implication of an empirical perspective is that reading fictional literature may not just be preferable as an entertainment vehicle but also be better at helping readers interact with other people and their social environments. Mar et al. (2006) argued, akin to the philosophical arguments above, that fiction readers may improve their social-inference skills through reading. The benefits of reading may even offset the social isolation inherent in reading. As Mar et al. noted, "Bookworms, by reading a great deal of narrative fiction, may buffer themselves from the effects of reduced direct interpersonal contact by simulating the social experiences depicted in stories" (Mar et al., 2006, p. 705). The plot and characterizations in novels and short stories can act as simulations of real-world situations. Regular and attentive reading of such stories may help the reader learn how to interact with similar character traits as well as how to respond to a given or similar situation depicted in a fictional work (Oatley, 1999). It may also help the reader develop empathy – a necessary trait in leaders and one of the key elements of emotional intelligence (Goleman, 1998).

Reading good fiction can also perhaps change how the reader perceives himself. In one study, researchers noted, in an experiment using Chekhov's short story *The Lady With the Toy Dog* as the source, that despite the setting of the story in a turn of the last century Russia, the reading of the story "changed (even if temporarily) how the readers, more than a century later, experienced their own personality traits" (Djikic, Oatley, Zoeterman, &

Peterson, 2009, p. 27). The assumption follows that reading can lead to a gradual change of self and to a better understanding of others (Djikic et al., 2009). As to the question of what kind of literature is most beneficial, the Djikic study also surmised that ". . . it appears important to consider that it may not be the sheer presence, but the quality of art-induced emotions – their complexity, depth, range, and intensity – that potentially facilitate the process of trait change" (p. 28).

In a related study, Johnson (2012) explored whether this effect on empathy carried over into real-world interactions. Johnson found that participants who read short stories "designed to induce compassionate feelings for the characters and model prosocial behavior" (p. 151) were significantly more likely to experience affective empathy in a real-world setting. He also found that prosocial behavior was an added benefit to reading fiction. Johnson concluded, ". . . it appears that 'curling up with a good book' may do more than provide relaxation and entertainment. Reading narrative fiction allows one to learn about our social world and as a result fosters empathic growth and prosocial behavior" (p. 154).

Good books help create good leaders

Great works of fiction, as Chesterton indicated, can also instruct and inspire people to do great things – to "slay dragons" as it were. Great literature may also quite literally make us better people – better able to navigate social relationships and circumstances encountered first through reading. Additionally, great works of fiction shows us that our own culture is not the sole repository of virtues and experiences. Fictional works, set in various times and cultures, display a wide array of universal characteristics and real-life experiences and create opportunities for the reader to experience and empathize with other cultures, the past and perhaps even prepare for coming events for novels set in the future.

Reading great fiction and even non-fiction enriches our lives, enhances our knowledge of the world around us, and can inspire us to do better in our personal and professional lives. Singh (1999) noted that "[the] Leadership role demands perspectives, worldviews, and beliefs; a passionate commitment to some values, ends, or, ultimate purposes balanced by a sense of responsibility and proportion that depends on listening to others, maintaining humility, and a sense of humour" (p. 3). Great literature was and remains a deep source of guidance for leaders and followers on how to live life well and in gaining perspectives and knowledge of other worldviews.

Sample (2001) astutely observed that people are what they read stating that "leaders should read and reread the supertexts as frequently as possible" (p. 3). Stories provide fresh perspectives, challenge assumptions, and even inform lived and shared experiences. A reader of great novels can vicariously live multiple lives in his or her lifetime.

Gosling and Villiers (2013) noted that "writers of fiction are able to present the inner musings and unconscious drives of their characters, as if they were observed events" providing profound insights on the angsts and joys associated with leadership that would otherwise be missed (p. 1). Great works of literature provide visceral insights to the emotional hardships of leadership not readily experienced in the leadership literature. Gosling and Villiers note that:

> Management theory is appallingly obscure about the experience of leading. Often the more positive aspects are emphasized – excitement, potency, moral courage, and the sense of achievement and affirmation. But loneliness, frustration, envy, disappointment and betrayal are probably ubiquitous and sometimes overwhelming aspects of a leader's life, yet are seldom mentioned, still less examined in any depth in standard leadership texts – and that includes the popular books supposedly written for practitioners as well as more abstract academic studies. One reason is that these experiences are difficult to study in real time, and leaders themselves are not always reliable informants about their interior lives and motives.
>
> (p. 1)

Seymour-Smith (1998) describes the power of great works of literature in that they "have changed or colored the ways in which people, even whole nations – as well as individuals – think of themselves" (p. xvii).

Good books capture and shape culture

Probably the best-known example of the concept that novels can shape culture is the contribution Harriet Beecher Stowe's 1851 novel *Uncle Tom's Cabin* made to the pre-Civil War abolition of slavery movement in the United States. Stowe's novel was released roughly, though in serial form, at the same time as *Moby-Dick* (Rosenthal, 2014, pp. 135–147). Stowe's depiction of slavery and the brutality of the institution, though seen by some today as problematic in its portrayal of African-Americans according to 1850s stereotypes, unquestionably humanized slaves in a way that newspaper articles, speeches, and sermons could not. Selling over 300,000 copies, the novel forced many Americans to feel empathy for people with whom most Americans would have thought they had nothing in common and ushered in a debate among the populace that generations of politicians had warped (Hagood, 2012, pp. 70–95). Stowe's searing novel undoubtedly helped shape antebellum culture and still stands as a prime example of the power of fictional narrative to capture and shape culture. Great literature is a primary vehicle by which cultures communicate, shape, and teach values to both their own culture and to the world more generally. In the case of *Uncle Tom's Cabin*, it communicated and reminded many readers at the time of the ideals that Americans often express publicly and privately, but often and grossly failed to live up to the ideals that "all men are created equal" and that all humans have a right to "life, liberty, and the pursuit of Happiness." Additionally, Stowe's novel communicated those values to those from other cultures and worldviews who might not understand the implications of the text of *The Declaration of Independence* but can gain an understanding of those ideals through their depiction in a novel.

Other examples of great literature that have shaped cultures include the *Bible* which was the impetus for many well-known charitable organizations like the Red Cross (U.S. and International), YMCA, the Salvation Army, not to mention the thousands of faith-based hospitals and schools around the United States and the world. Additionally, muckraking journalist Upton Sinclair's 1904 novel *The Jungle* – a harrowing tale of a Lithuanian immigrant working in Chicago's meatpacking industry – is often credited with inspiring a change in America's food regulatory regime. Sinclair's vivid and often grotesque images of the unsanitary, brutal, and dehumanizing working conditions in the Chicago meatpacking industry inspired a widespread call for tighter regulations for health and worker safety issues. Similar to *Uncle Tom's Cabin*, *The Jungle* humanized a group of people mostly unknown to many Americans and emphasized the often awful conditions of a growing meatpacking industry whose product more and more Americans were using. Those images brought home the dangers to personal and food safety and provided an impetus to cultural and political change.

Summary and conclusion

Good novels are mirrors. They challenge the readers' objective sense of self and safely obligate them to examine their lives in relation to the people, events, and themes in the stories of others. Ultimately, readers of great novels adjust their personal narratives based upon the lessons gleaned from great authors. In this manner, reading great novels becomes a shortcut to developing emotional, social, and cultural intelligence, good character, and discernment.

Good narratives are also windows. They not only shape readers, but they can nudge culture by attaching emotions to facts, people, and places.

Great literature explores universal themes and values that capture the zeitgeist and anchor esteemed values in a society's meta-narrative. They also critique a society's cherished values and virtues through vivid plots with relatable protagonists and identifiable antagonists to move readers to think and act better.

The next chapter delves into the three works chosen as exemplars: *Don Quixote*, *Moby-Dick*, and *Pride and Prejudice*. It shows how and why those works are considered almost universally to be classics of the form. The chapter will also prime the uninitiated on how to be connoisseurs of great literature. Chapter 2 is primarily provided to give context for Chapter 3, which makes explicit connections between these great books, great novels generally, and to the study and practice of leadership.

Notes

1 Various literary critics describe three, seven, nine, etc. basic plot points for all narrative literature. From there, the debate expands to a variety of relatively arcane critical approaches such as psychology and other perspectives of literary criticism that go beyond what the average consumer of great literature will encounter in the search for his or her next great read. The goal of this book is to encourage leaders to read great works and to equip them to be connoisseurs of great literature from a layperson's view; not that of a PhD level literary critic (though a few are quoted in this book).
2 While the earliest Western novel is often thought to be Cervantes's *Don Quixote* (or other works) appearing in the 16th century AD, the earliest novel in the world is thought by many (though not universally so) to be a Japanese work entitled *The Tale of Genji* by a noblewoman named Murasaki Shikibu published around 1020 AD, though no original manuscript exists.
3 Johannes Gutenberg is generally considered to be the inventor of "the printing press" though forms of printing like woodblocks and the like had been in existence in China and other places for centuries. The printing press revolutionized many aspects of European culture: politics, religion, education and not least the spread of books in vernacular European languages instead of mostly or solely in Latin or Greek.

References

Aristotle. (trans. 1996). *Poetics*. (M. Heath, Trans.) London, England: Penguin Classics.

Austen, J. (1813/2003). *Pride and prejudice*. Barnes & Noble Classics.

Battles, M. (2006). Introduction. In R. de Bury (ed.), *The Love of Books: The Philobiblon of Richard de Bury* (pp. vii–xi). New York, NY: Barnes and Noble Publishers.

Baym, N. (1979). Melville's Quarrel with Fiction. *PMLA*, *94*(5), 909–923. https://doi.org/10.2307/461973

Carroll, N. (1994). The Paradox of Junk Fiction. *Journal of Philosophy and Literature, 18*(2), 225–241.

Chesterton, G. K. (1909/2006). *Tremendous trifles*. Project Gutenberg Literary Archive Foundation.

de Bury, R. (1344/2009). *The Philobiblon* (M. Battles, Trans.) New York, NY: Barnes and Noble Publishers (Originally published in 1344).

Djikic, M., Oatley, K., Zoeterman, S., & Peterson, J. B. (2009). On being moved by art: How reading fiction transforms the self. *Creativity Research Journal, 21*(1), 24–29.

Goleman, D. (1998). What makes a leader? *Harvard Business Review, 76*, 93–102.

Gosling, J. & Villiers, P. (2013). *Fictional leaders: Heroes, villains and absent friends*. New York, NY: Palgrave Macmillan.

Griswold, C. J. (2006). *Imagination: Morals Science and Arts*. Cambridge, UK: Cambridge University Press.

Hagood, T. C. (2012). "Oh, what a slanderous book": Reading Uncle Tom's Cabin in the Antebellum South. *Southern Quarterly: A Journal of the Arts in the South, 49*(4), 71–93.

Heath, M. (1996). *Introduction in Poetics by Aristotle* (pp. vii–lxxi). London, England: Penguin Classics.

Hipple, T. (1992). Young adult literature and the test of time. *Publishing Research Quarterly, 8*, 5–13.

Johnson, D. R. (2012). Transportation into a story increases empathy, prosocial behavior, and perceptual bias toward fearful expressions. *Personality and Individual Differences, 52*(2), 150–155.

Lewis, C. S. (1944/1970). *On the reading of old books*. Grand Rapids, MI: William B. Eerdmans Publishing.

Mar, R. A., Oatley, K., Hirsh, J., de la Paz, J., & Peterson, J. B. (2006). Bookworms versus nerds: Exposure to fiction versus non-fiction, divergent associations with social ability, and the simulation of fictional social worlds. *Journal of Research in Personality, 40*(5), 694–712. https://doi.org/10.1016/j.jrp.2005.08.002

Nussbaum, M. (1995). *Poetic justice: The literary imagination and public life*. Boston, MA: Beacon Press.

Oatley, K. (1999). Why fiction may be twice as true as fact: Fiction as cognitive and emotional simulation. *Review of General Psychology, 3*(2), 101–117. https://doi.org/10.1037/1089-2680.3.2.101

Prior, K. S. (2018). *On reading well: Finding the good life through great books*. Ada, MI: Brazos Press.

Rosenthal, D. (2014). The sentimental appeal to salvific paternity in "Uncle Tom's Cabin" and "Moby-Dick." *Texas Studies in Literature and Language, 56*(2), 135.

Sample, S. (2001). *The contrarian's guide to leadership*. San Francisco, CA: Jossey-Bass.

Seymour-Smith, M. (1998). *The 100 most influential books ever written: The history of thought from ancient times to today*. New York, NY: Barnes & Noble Books.

Schopenhauer, A. (1851/1882). *Essays of Arthur Schopenhauer* (R. Dircks, Trans.). University of Adelaide: eBooks@adelaide. Retrieved November 1, 2018 from https://ebooks.adelaide.edu.au/s/schopenhauer/arthur/essays/index.html

Shakespeare, N. (2016). *Which of today's novelists will stand the test of time?* Retrieved November 1, 2018, from https://www.telegraph.co.uk/books/what-to-read/which-of-todays-novelists-will-stand-the-test-of-time/

Singh, S. P. (1999). Learning leadership and decision-making from literature. *Vikalpa*, *24*(3), 3–10. https://doi.org/10.1177/0256090919990302

Smith, A. (1759/1976). *The Theory of Moral Sentiments*. Oxford, UK: Oxford University Press.

2 *Don Quixote*, *Moby-Dick*, and *Pride and Prejudice*

Exemplars

Don Quixote, *Moby-Dick*, and *Pride and Prejudice* have stood the "test of time." They are often, if not universally, recognized as among the greatest works of narrative fiction from the past five centuries. Each novel and its respective author will, in turn, be highlighted, summarized, and discussed in terms of its general insights. As the subsequent chapter will focus more directly on leadership themes from each novel, this chapter serves to orientate the readers to the respective themes, plots, and characters. These three novels: *Don Quixote* by Miguel de Cervantes Saavedra, *Pride and Prejudice* by Jane Austen, and *Moby-Dick* by Herman Melville are a modest sample of great novels from which leaders and followers can read to broaden their experiences while also being entertained by great characters, distant and exotic settings, plots, and times.

The brief overview of each novel also includes some historical context and biography of the authors. The review of the time periods of the writing of great novels illustrates how novels can serve as commentaries on contemporary society. In this fashion, novels can provide reflective public critiques to help contemporary readers step outside their respective cultures and objectively evaluate their role and place in society. For modern readers, they provide history lessons and a mechanism by which to evaluate current customs, laws, and attitudes. Knowledge of the historical insights of the times and places in the novels also equip readers to better discern the different, and at times subtle, messages in a given story. A lesson for leaders is, like great authors, that their work narratives are didactic commentaries on the organizational mission, values, and conditions.

The brief biography of the authors provides the connoisseurs of literature insights to each author's experiences, motives, and abilities that inevitably show up in the novel. In one sense, all novels are a bit autobiographical in that they reflect something about the author. Knowing the life and times of the authors not only puts the respective narratives in context but also allows the authors to become additional protagonists alongside those in their corresponding novel, thus providing another life for readers to learn and grow from. A lesson for leaders is, like authors, to recognize that their personality cannot but help shape and reinforce (or undermine) the credibility of any organizational narrative.

Don Quixote

As noted in the previous chapter, Seymour-Smith (1998) described the power of great works of fiction noting that they "have changed or colored the ways in which people, even whole nations – as well as individuals – think of themselves" (p. xvii). He listed *Don Quixote* as one such novel. The transformational effect of literature is itself a central theme of Cervantes's *Don Quixote*. By reading chivalric romances, the character of Don Quixote emerges from his otherwise routine life to become his own protagonist – a knight-errant determined to "change the world and right wrongs."

A prerequisite to being a connoisseur of literature that is translated is recognizing how meanings and nuances such as puns and double entendres can be lost in the process. Cervantes's sophistication as a writer and the heart of *Don Quixote's* message can be incomplete when relying on English translations from the original 17th-century Spanish. The principle of *traduttore traditore* – "the translator is the traitor" – holds that no matter how conscientious the translator, translations of literature naturally involve some small distortions of the original, especially when it comes to humor, imagery, and poetry (Caponegro, 2008). *Don Quixote's* setting in its historical context provides additional richness of meaning to different expressions and references somewhat lost on modern audiences. At the same time, while not always able to fully capture the nuanced meanings in *Don Quixote*, the art and science of interpretation allows the translators, and thus the readers, to capture the essence of Cervantes's intentions.

Considered by many to be the first modern novel, Miguel de Cervantes's (1547–1616) *Don Quixote* continues to be recognized as one of the great novels worldwide over 500 years after its publication. Not only is it in Harold Bloom's (1994/2014) *The Western Canon*, but it is also included in Seymour-Smith's (1998) *The 100 Most Influential Books Ever Written: The History of Thought from Ancient Times to Today*. In 2002, a list of the 100 world's best authors and books from 54 countries listed *Don Quixote* as the world's best book (Chrisafis, 2002). Greenberg (2004) characterized *Don Quixote* as "the mother of all novels," and as American literary critic Lionel Trilling (1953) noted, "All prose fiction is a variation on the theme of *Don Quixote*" (p. 203). The story of *Don Quixote* transcends generations and cultures to provide timeless lessons for the lay reader as well as for aspiring and established leaders.

There are ongoing academic debates about the best way to interpret Cervantes's novel. Hart (2009) demonstrated how *Don Quixote* was originally considered a "funny book" while more recent readers see the story as more of a tragedy. Wardropper (1965) argued that it is a didactic pseudo-history. Greenberg (2004) distinguished between two schools of thought for rightly understanding *Don Quixote:* the Comedists and the Profundists. Stavans (2005) noted that:

> Over the years, *Don Quixote* has been a template of the times: The 18th century believe the knight to be a lunatic, lost to reason; The Victorians approached him as a romantic dreamer, trapped, just like artists and prophets, in his own fantasy; the modernist applauded his quest for an inner language; the postmodernists adore his dislocated identity. Psychiatrists have seen him as a case study in schizophrenia. Communists have turned him into a victim of market forces. Intellectual historians have portrayed him as a portent of Spain's decline into intellectual obscurantism.
>
> (p. B11)

Ormsby (1885), who provided an English translation of *Don Quixote*, observed the following:

> It is plain that "Don Quixote" was generally regarded at first, and indeed in Spain for a long time, as little more than a queer droll book, full of laughable incidents and absurd situations, very amusing, but not entitled to much consideration or care. All the editions printed in Spain from 1637 to 1771, when the famous printer Ibarra took it up, were mere trade editions, badly and carelessly printed on vile paper and got up in the style of chapter-books intended only for popular use, with, in most cases, uncouth illustrations and clap-trap additions by the publisher . . . .
>
> The zeal of publishers, editors, and annotators brought about a remarkable change of sentiment with regard to *Don Quixote*. A vast number of its admirers began to grow ashamed of laughing over it. It became almost a crime to treat it as a humorous book. The humour was not entirely denied, but, according to the new view, it was rated as an altogether secondary quality, a mere accessory, nothing more than the stalking-horse under the presentation of which Cervantes shot his philosophy or his satire, or whatever it was he meant to shoot; for on this point opinions varied. All were agreed, however, that the object he aimed at was not the books of chivalry. He said emphatically in the preface to the First Part and in the last sentence of the Second, that he had no other object in view than to discredit these books, and this, to advanced criticism, made it clear that his object must have been something else.

Whether Cervantes's conscious intent was to discredit and discourage readers away from the idle reading of chivalric novels or merely a pretext for other agendas so as to make it past the royal censors,[1] the book comments on multiple themes that resonate with contemporary and modern audiences. In lieu of discerning Cervantes's motives and original intent for writing *Don Quixote*, this chapter explores a few general themes from the text. Cervantes provided readers with wisdom about the "good life" through the adventures and misadventures of Don Quixote. The book abounds with life lessons and morals that celebrate the passionate pursuit of virtue and gallantry illustrating to the reader that one does not need a formal title of nobility such as "Don" to think and behave nobly.[2] It is in this vein that Cervantes's *Don Quixote* is a commentary on wisdom. The novel is filled with over 200 proverbs and numerous lengthy soliloquies, commentaries, and examples relating to discernment and doing good. Don Quixote's words to Sancho near the end of the book reveal one of Cervantes's ambitions for his readers – "what I have said to you thus far has been in the nature of instructions for the adornment of the soul."[3]

Brief historical context

In the late 15th and early 16th centuries, Spain rose from centuries of Moorish rule and asserted itself as a world empire through its exploration of the known and the New World beginning in 1492. Less than a century later, through a series of political, cultural, and economic changes, the Spanish empire reached its zenith. In 1588, the British defeated the Spanish Armada, initiating, according to some historians, a gradual diminution of Spanish global power over the next couple of centuries. It was during this time, just past the apex of Spanish dominance, that Cervantes penned *Don Quixote*. It was also a time of widening disparity between the haves and the have-nots (Ife, 2002, pp. 11–31). The massive influx of wealth from Central and South America not only made many Spaniards wealthy but also caused rampant inflation aggravating the poverty of many peasants. Sheep farming and agriculture in La Mancha proved to be a major industry bringing relative stability to the country. This stability was rocked by famine beginning in 1590 and by an outbreak of bubonic plague. Ife (2002) pointed out the numerous prosperous farmers that populated Cervantes's novel, despite Don Quixote's self-characterization as lacking wealth. According to Napierkowski and Stanley (2000), the religious demographics of the 16th century also impacted the concepts set forth in the novel: "while the rest of Europe is undergoing a period known as the Renaissance, Spain clings to its medieval values" (p. 69). Perhaps this explains why Cervantes felt the need to address the influence of chivalric novels and the idealistic fantasies they presented.

The Spanish Inquisition also shaped the culture of Spain during Cervantes's lifetime. Their censorship of publications, particularly any literature that criticized the monarchy or the Church, probably explains Cervantes's style of ambiguity, absurdity, and irony to evade the censors of the time (Layson & Carman, 2013). In the interest of suppressing religious differences from Spain and uniting the country under Counter Reformation Catholicism, the Habsburgs (the Spanish royal dynasty at the time) also expelled the Moriscos – the Christian descendants of Moorish Muslims expelled during the Reconquista a century earlier. In a matter of five years (1609–1614), approximately 300,000 people were deported to North Africa by King Philip III (Layson & Carman, 2013).

The region of La Mancha, chosen by Cervantes as the backdrop for his novel, was not a noteworthy place. Layson and Carman (2013) cited literary critic Johnson who commented:

> la mancha means 'stain' in Spanish, and is the name of a region with nothing particular to recommend it: no cities, no illustrious families, the site of no important historical events, a semiarid plain given over mostly to wheat and dotted with windmills.
>
> (p. 3)

It seems that Cervantes chose an otherwise ordinary territory for Don Quixote's extraordinary adventures. Cervantes's choice of such a prosaic un-Romantic locale highlights the absurdity of the "Man of La Mancha's" misadventures. Hailing from "La Mancha" could be seen as being a "stain" on Don Quixote's honor, teaching that one's humble origins do not necessarily determine one's destiny. A similar lesson is part of the theme of *Pride and Prejudice* not to mention the real-life example of US President Abraham Lincoln, discussed in a later chapter, who is famed for coming from humble "log cabin" beginnings in rural Kentucky and Illinois to rise to the most powerful office in the land.

Brief biography of Miguel de Cervantes

Born in 1547 to a poor doctor, Miguel de Cervantes received a modicum of education from a schoolmaster "who was permeated by the new critical spirit" of the age. At 22, most likely fleeing a warrant for dueling and a potential punishment of having his right hand cut off and ten years imprisonment, he fled Madrid and ultimately ended up in Rome (McCrory, 2014). When war with the Turks broke out, Cervantes joined the military to redeem himself from his legal troubles. He was wounded three times by the Ottoman-Turks during the decisive sea battle at Lepanto suffering a permanent injury to his left hand (McCrory, 2014). He fought until 1575 when, on his return voyage to Spain, he was captured by Algerian pirates who imprisoned and enslaved him. Five years later, he was released on ransom and returned to Spain a hero. His military exploits and imprisonment were obliquely chronicled in Part One of *Don Quixote* in three chapters often referred to as "The Captive's Tale."

Despite his notoriety, Cervantes returned home poor and without a job from the Crown – the usual reward for a returning war hero. In 1587, as a provisioning agent for the Spanish Armada (preparing for its 1588 action against England), he was excommunicated for a short time for seizing corn from Church property, even though ordered to do so by the king (McCrory, 2014). During the 1590s, Cervantes wrote a few nondescript works, was a commissary agent, and worked as a tax collector. He went to jail on more than one occasion for lending out his tax collections at interest and various other minor offenses. It was during this troubled time that the story of *Don Quixote* was born. At the novel's publication in 1604, Cervantes became both wealthy and well known around the world. He completed the promised second part of the novel shortly before his death, the same month William Shakespeare passed, in April of 1616 (McCrory, 2014).

Main characters

Alonso Quixano. He is a hidalgo (low-level gentry) of La Mancha, Spain and the main character and delusional hero of the novel. He lives in a fantasy world. His love for stories of chivalry drives his quest to resurrect the chivalric values and play the role of knight-errant. Taking the name Don Quixote, de la Mancha, he embarks on daring adventures sparked by his own imagination setting into motion adventures that allow for the contemplation and display of noble-minded thinking and behavior. He also drafts his broken down barn horse Rocinante to be his noble steed.

Sancho Panza. Sancho is chosen by Don Quixote to be his faithful squire. He is the quintessential sidekick who serves as Don Quixote's assistant, sounding board, and often ambivalent pupil. Sancho also represents common sense and the peasantry in Cervantes's time. Although aware of Don Quixote's delusional state, Sancho remains loyal to the end.

Teresa Panza. Sancho Panza's wife. She is loyal and solid like her husband. She stays with the couple's two children as Sancho accompanies Don Quixote on his adventures.

Dulcinea del Toboso. Don Quixote declares Dulcinea to be the love of his life and "mistress of his thoughts." She is the motivation behind Quixote's many escapades and chivalric behavior. She is ignorant of Quixote's love for her. Nevertheless Don Quixote imagines that she reciprocates his love. She is his muse.

Barber (Master Nicolás). He is a close friend of Don Quixote who desires to restore Quixote to sanity by convincing him to forget and get rid of his books of chivalry and thus his foolish notions of being a knight-errant. The barber also remains a faithful friend to the end staying with Quixote even to his final hours.

Curate (Pedro Perez). The Curate, friend of the barber and also of Don Quixote, assists the barber in their plan to disguise themselves in an attempt to restore Don Quixote's sanity.

Second Innkeeper. He gives lodging to Don Quixote, Sancho, the curate and the barber on multiple occasions. Like Quixote, he enjoys reading stories of chivalry but does not take them as seriously so as to attempt to live them out as does Quixote. He indulges Don Quixote by playing along with his madness.

Friston. Friston appears to be Quixote's chief enemy, an enchanter who foils Quixote. Don Quixote accuses him of stealing his library and also of transforming the giants Quixote attacks into windmills thus robbing him of the glory he seeks.

Samson Carrasco. He is a young bachelor (synonymous for young scholar) and malevolent friend. He goes along with Quixote's fantasy of being a knight-errant with enthusiasm and provides him with adventure, even to the point of disguising himself as a knight and battling Don Quixote.

The Duke and Duchess. They are a noble couple that goes to great lengths to treat Don Quixote as the knight he thinks himself to be but do so for their own amusement. They are greatly entertained by Sancho and Quixote's behavior and adventures, indulging Quixote in his delusions to the point of excess.

The Noble Thief (Roque Guinart). Guinart is the captain of a band of thieves. In one episode he and his gang came to the aid of a young woman in distress after which he fairly divided her belongings among his squires. Don Quixote wondered how such a man whose lifestyle revolves around robbery could be capable of noble ideas and actions.

Synopsis of Don Quixote

After reading numerous chivalric novels, Don Quixote, the man from La Mancha, Spain, sets out on his old barn horse, Rocinante, as a knight-errant convinced it is his mission to defend the defenseless and live the values of chivalry found in his books. His faithful squire Sancho Panza rides with him while also trying to keep him grounded in reality, though Sancho often ends up playing along with Quixote's outlandish fantasies. Although Quixote fails in many of his adventures, he continues to persevere in his quest to defend the weak while winning the hand of his lady love Dulcinea del Toboso. Commentary on social, political, and religious concepts in Cervantes's Spain runs throughout the lengthy tale of adventures and misadventures. The novel concludes with Quixote's late realization that he is not actually a knight-errant, and that he has been living in a fantasy world. On his deathbed, he renounces his books of chivalry and his imaginary quest and dies peacefully surrounded by his faithful friends.

Main themes

The general themes, as with all great literature, help "adorn the soul." As Don Quixote noted to his loyal squire Sancho Panza:

> If you follow these precepts and rules, Sancho, your days will be long, your fame eternal, your rewards abundant, your happiness indescribable.
>
> The instructions I have so far given you are for the embellishment of your soul. Listen now to some that will serve you for the adornment of your body.
>
> (Cervantes, 1604/1956, p. 740)

Reality and fantasy

So impactful was the story of Don Quixote that his very name has become an English adjective. *The Oxford English Dictionary* defines the adjective "quixotic" as "Of an action, attribute, idea, etc.: characteristic of or appropriate to Don Quixote; demonstrating or motivated by exaggerated notions of chivalry and romanticism; naively idealistic; unrealistic, impracticable; (also) unpredictable, capricious, whimsical."

The novel is chock-a-block with the interplay and confusion of reality with fantasy. George Bernard Shaw wrote, "The reasonable man adapts himself to the world: the unreasonable one persists in trying to adapt the world to himself. Therefore all progress depends on the unreasonable man" (Shaw, 1903). Cervantes and Shaw recognized that perhaps one needs to be a little unreasonable and perhaps seemingly crazy if he or she is going to change or advance the world. *Don Quixote* provides a story and language for a conversation about that space between heroic and foolish pursuits – between the reality of a particular situation and whether the proposed course of action is realistic or too far "out there."

Social class and character

Cervantes used Don Quixote's adventures to consistently, and not always gently, probe and explore the inconsistencies between one's class and one's character. In this, Sancho Panza is the archetypal example of the paradox of low class and high character. Sancho and his wife belong to the peasant class in Spain. Despite, or maybe because of, this station, Cervantes portrayed Sancho Panza as consistently solid, grounded, honest, and loyal to a fault. While Don Quixote is given to flights of fancy, the Panzas are mostly grounded in reality and common sense. This period of Spanish history saw a transition from older ideals of romance, chivalry and love for more prosaic ideals of efficiency and practicality. Sancho believes somewhat in both and acts as a kind of bridge between the two. Don Quixote is clearly pushed to the chivalric model by his literary immersion in tales of knights and derring-do.

Moby-Dick by Herman Melville

When first released, *Moby-Dick* generated mixed, mostly negative, reviews and dismal sales in both England and America, leaving Melville confused and poor (Paretsky, 1999). Not until the 1920s did *Moby-Dick* rise to prominence in the American canon after a Melville revival (Brooks, 1915). Van Wyck Brooks, a prolific and astute literary historian, critic, and biographer called on writers to create a unique American literary identity and a usable past. He even suggested that they begin with the study of Herman Melville, who had been "so neglected" by Americans. Raymond Weaver answered that call and published *Herman Melville: Man, Mariner and Mystic* in 1921 to become the progenitor of the Melville revival. Gander (2010) noted that

> The reason for Melville's revival was arguably due to a confluence of cultural and social needs and anxieties. Melville's sea-tales, laced with autobiography and the observations of the participant author, provided personalized narrative of adventure that imposed form upon experience.
>
> (p. 760)

Gander went on to explain Melville's resurrection. Spanning two world wars and the Great Depression, the "Melville Revival" took shape during an extended period of cultural and economic crisis. Many of Melville's works represented a fusion of fiction and fact, and as such, spoke to those Americans who were driven by the need "to explain things, to make one's own experience, and the world around that experience comprehensible" (Gander, 2010, p. 760).

Moby-Dick, provided a symbolic commentary on the social walls that the New England religion, industrialization, and expansion had established and man's subsequent alienation from nature. Melville's detailed scientific information on whales and the nature of whaling to reveal that the illusion that while science may provide a god-like sense of understanding and control, humans are not omniscient and omnipotent. The almost prophetic warnings embedded in the metaphysical themes made Melville's opus unwelcomed in his own time, only to be valued in a Melville revival 70 years later as a usable past.

Historical context

As with previous Melville novels, *Moby-Dick* contained elements of historical fact to resonate with contemporary readers. *Moby-Dick* appeared while the United States was in the throes of the slavery debates that would culminate in the Civil War in the 1860s. The Industrial Revolution was also in full force and as noted by Armstrong (2004), Ishmael "rhapsodizes about the contributions made to America's economy and the dissemination of its influence by the vast whaling fleet, which at the apogee of the industry, spanned the globe" (p. 1039). Melville used many images of machinery and the factory in reference to the ship and the whales. A common understanding of the novel is as an allegory of humankind's quest to conquer nature and its power and limitations. Captain Ahab's quest for the white whale – whaling generally – is often understood as humans using technology in an attempt to subdue nature (Armstrong, 2004, p. 1042). By 1850, the American whaling industry was nearing its apex and New Bedford, Massachusetts had replaced Nantucket as its center, albeit short-lived. The coming discovery of petroleum in Titusville, Pennsylvania in 1859 eliminated the need for whale oil. Additionally, the transcontinental railroad in the 1860s obviated the need for an East Coast portage and San Francisco replaced the Atlantic coast as the more convenient port for Pacific and Arctic whaling fleets. These factors, among other things, would usher in whaling's eventual decline, but the 1840s and 1850s were heady times for whalers. Ever present danger and profits were common aspects of life for New Bedford whalers in the 1840s.

The *Pequod*'s racially diverse crew was somewhat emblematic of a relatively common phenomenon in the first half of the 19th century. While white Americans held a strong stereotype that Native Americans were mostly fit to be harpooners (Tashtego's job on the *Pequod*), Native Americans often rose to the officer ranks on whaling vessels. Whaling was one of the few areas where Native Americans could rise above what were generally poor social and economic opportunities. That Melville limits Tashtego, Queequeg, and Daggoo to their roles as harpooners in some ways fails to reflect the reality that, compared to society at large, whaling offered more opportunities for profit and positions of authority to men of color (Shoemaker, 2013).

True to form for Herman Melville, *Moby-Dick* paralleled real-life events. Melville had known about the tragedy of the *Essex*[4] having read Owen Chase's version in *The Narrative*. Melville picked up additional details and lore about the tragedy. It was part of the conversation on the *Acushnet's* crew as they entered the South Seas, where the *Essex* sank on November 20, 1820, as a result of a sperm whale attack. Melville was also familiar with an 1839 article by Jeremiah Reynolds titled, *Mocha Dick: Or, the White Whale of the Pacific*, a true story about a large albino whale off the coast of Chile (Parker, 1996).

Brief biography – Herman Melville

Herman Melville was 32 years old when he published *Moby-Dick* in 1851. He had already sailed on merchant, whaling, and naval ships, briefly lived as a castaway on a Polynesian island, and published five semi-autobiographical seafaring novels. While he earned modest royalties from his first two books and mixed reviews for his other three, Melville held various jobs before and after the publication of *Moby-Dick* to support his wife and four children. Even though he was a relatively popular American author upon *Moby-Dick*'s release, he could not sustain a living as a writer and would die in relative obscurity (Howard, 1950).

Herman Melville grew up in relative prosperity for his first 11 years as both his mother and father came from prominent and well-established families. He had formal and informal tutors prior to attending the New York Male School and Albany Academy where he received a classical and practical education. A dramatic reversal of fortune in the family introduced Melville to the vicissitudes of life and marked the beginning of his "real" education. His father's lack of business savvy and poor timing required that the Melville family flee under the cover of the night to avoid creditors and live in Albany under the charity of relatives (Parker, 1996). Fourteen months later his father died in January of 1832 requiring him to take a job as a bank clerk, a job he would hold into 1834 when he then went to work for his older brother.

At the age of 19 and out of necessity, Herman took his first sea voyage on a merchant vessel to and from Liverpool in the summer of 1839. Two years later, he would return to the sea after a brief stint as a teacher and when travel out west to extended family failed to provide an adequate living. In January 1841, Melville set sail on the whaler *Acushnet* out of New Bedford. After 18 months at sea the *Acushnet* harbored at a Polynesian island where Melville chose to spend the next four months. Those experiences would be the basis of his first novel, *Typee*. In August of 1842, he joined the crew of an Australian whaler, the *Lucy Ann,* only to land in Tahiti with a brief stay in jail for accusations of mutiny, which provided the context for his second novel, *Omoo*. In November, he signed on as temporary harpooner with the *Charles & Henry* until the ship reached Hawaii in May, 1843. While working as a clerk and taking in the history of the islands, Herman got homesick and joined the US Navy to get a ride home. His first-hand experience on the man-of-war and with navy traditions was the fodder for his fifth novel, *White Jacket*. Seven months later, at the age of 23, on October 3, 1844, Herman returned to Massachusetts (Parker, 1996).

In 1847, he stayed with extended family, whose financial situations had improved since leaving over three and half years earlier. His family encouraged him to put the tales of his adventures to pen and provided the impetus for his writing career (Parker, 1996). Herman married Elizabeth Shaw in 1847, a daughter of the prominent Lemuel Shaw, Chief Justice of the Supreme Court of Massachusetts and longtime friend of Melville's father. Herman and Liz relocated to Pittsfield, Massachusetts where they met and become friends with Nathaniel Hawthorne.

Unfortunately, mounting debts from his waning popularity ended the Melvilles' idyllic life and they relocated to New York City in 1863 with their four children. Melville took a job as a customs inspector on the New York docks, a job he held for 20 years. He continued his writing and ventured into poetry with little success. The last decades for the Melville family were apparently filled with despair and disappointment corresponding to Melville's reportedly reclusive and volatile temperament (Renker, 2014), almost mirroring the metaphysical despair so much emphasized in *Moby-Dick* (Renker, 2014). Melville passed away on September 28, 1891, at the age of 72. The *New York Times* obituary dated October 2, 1891, described him as "a man who is so little known" and for whom it was difficult to comprehend the reason for a "speedy oblivion by which a once famous man so long survived his fame."

Main characters

Ishmael. He is the narrator of the novel and a sharp observer. He forms a close friendship with Queequeg and is initially leery of Captain Ahab and his motives. He eventually succumbs to Ahab's spell like the rest of the crew of the *Pequod*.

Captain Ahab. Ahab's mad maniacal quest to seek and destroy the giant sperm whale Moby Dick dominates the plot of the novel. Single-minded, desperate, hateful, and driven – he leads the crew to ultimate destruction. Ahab had been scarred physically and spiritually during a previous encounter with Moby Dick.

Queequeg. Queequeg is a Polynesian harpooner who befriends Ishmael at the beginning of the novel. He is a loyal friend, helps Ishmael broaden his own horizons, and is an expert harpooner. He saves Ishmael's life at the end of the novel.

Father Mapple. His sermon on the Book of Jonah[5] at the Whaleman's Chapel sets the tone for the novel. The sermon, about denying one's own desires for a higher calling provides a direct foil to Ahab's single-minded selfish and destructive ambitions.

Fedallah. He is a mysterious and seemingly ancient Indian or Zoroastrian "fire worshipper" who is Ahab's harpooner and spiritual guide. Melville calls him Ahab's "Dark Shadow." He predicts Ahab's death foreshadowing the end of the *Pequod* and her crew.

Starbuck. Starbuck is a devout Quaker and the chief mate aboard the *Pequod*. He vainly attempts to dissuade Ahab from his destructive obsession. Starbuck even contemplates arresting Ahab, though he eventually decides his obligations lie with the Captain.

Stubb. Stubb is the always present second mate. He is constantly picking on Fleece, the cook, often has a smile on his face, and has an ever-present pipe.

Flask. Flask is the third mate and an aggressive whale hunter.

Tashtego. Tashtego is the harpooner on Stubb's boat. He is a Wampanoag Indian.

Daggoo. Daggoo is an African from a coastal village. He is portrayed as almost regal by Melville.

Bildad. Bildad is a hypocritical Quaker and co-owner of the *Pequod*.

Moby Dick. He is the titular white whale that is the focus of Ahab's mad quest. Though a beast, Melville imbues the whale with malicious intent seemingly on the prowl for Ahab and other whalers.

Synopsis

As the novel begins, Ishmael, the novel's narrator, travels from New York to Massachusetts in hopes of finding work aboard a whaling ship. Since he is unable to make it on the ferry to Nantucket in time, he stays in a run-down hotel. There he meets Queequeg, a tattooed harpooner. Ishmael first sees Queequeg as a "savage," but soon, the two become close friends after spending some days at the hotel. The two eventually set off for Nantucket together. Ishmael makes a deal with Bildad and Peleg, owners of the *Pequod*, for Queequeg and him to be whalers aboard the ship. At this time, Ishmael learns that the captain of the *Pequod*, Ahab, has recently lost his leg to a great white whale called Moby Dick.

The *Pequod* sets sail from Nantucket on Christmas day. Ishmael describes Starbuck, the first mate, and his almost superstitious belief that man should fear whales, making him one of the more cautious men aboard the ship. After some time has passed aboard the *Pequod*, Ahab finally shows himself on deck. Melville characterizes Ahab as mentally troubled, and it soon becomes plain that he is on a mission to hunt down and kill Moby Dick, the whale who took his leg. He sees Moby Dick as evil and charges the crew with the task of looking for the whale, offering a gold doubloon reward to the first crewmember to spot the great white whale.

When the crew first lowers the harpoon boats in pursuit of a whale, a group of men emerge from the hold – Ahab's private crew hired to help him hunt Moby Dick. Up to this point, none of the crew knew of their presence on the ship. When the crew catches and kills its first whale, Ishmael gives detailed depictions of the appearance of whales as well as the process of cutting open a whale carcass. As the *Pequod* encounters other ships, Ahab always asks the captain if he has news of the location of Moby Dick. Ahab's thirst for vengeance against the great whale is clearly an obsession, and Ahab is depicted as somewhat mad in his quest.

Ishmael describes several rumors and superstitions surrounding Moby Dick, and throughout the novel furthers suspense surrounding this seemingly uncatchable whale. Furthermore, on several occasions, Ishmael describes whales and whaling to the reader, seemingly in an effort to understand whales. He goes into great detail, even comparing the head of a sperm whale with the head of a right whale as the two heads are positioned on either end of the *Pequod*, keeping the ship balanced. As the *Pequod* continues to capture more whales, Pip, the cabin boy, jumps out of his harpooning boat in fear, and to teach him a lesson, Stubb (the second mate) leaves him there. His experience being left alone in the sea drives him mad, and he becomes a constant companion at Ahab's side. Ishmael continues describing various aspects of whaling and life at sea, and the *Pequod* comes upon the *Samuel Enderby*, another ship whose captain has lost a limb (his arm) to Moby Dick. The two captains are friendly at first and share a toast, but when Boomer, the captain of the *Enderby*, thinks Ahab crazy to continue chasing the great white whale, Ahab leaves abruptly. At this point, Ahab's drive for revenge is clearly affecting his mental state – he is coming unhinged. He has to balance his own pursuit of Moby Dick with keeping the crew in his good graces, so that they will still be willing to go after the whale should the *Pequod* ever come upon it.

Finally, the *Pequod* meets Moby Dick. All of the harpooning boats set off in pursuit, and the great whale surfaces directly beneath Ahab's boat, sending its crew into the water. With skilled maneuvering from Starbuck, the men are rescued and the chase begins again. Similarly, Ahab and several crewmembers are again thrown into the water by the whale and one, Fedallah, dies. A third chase commences, and this time, Ahab gets tangled in the lines and does not make it. Moby Dick smashes the *Pequod*, and it sinks, creating a vortex that sucks down everyone and everything, except for Ishmael. The only reason he survives is that he was thrown far from the *Pequod* and Ahab's harpoon boat during the wreck. As the novel ends, another whaling ship picks up Ishmael while floating on a coffin originally made for the then ailing Queequeg.

Main themes

Hubris

The related dangers of obsession and hubris are throughout the novel. Akin to *Don Quixote*; *Moby Dick*'s main plot is so impactful that it has spawned dozens, if not hundreds of copies, homages, et al. To chase one's "white whale" is synonymous with the destructive, single-minded all-consuming focus on one goal. Melville didn't invent the theme of course, but he is largely responsible for embedding that turn of phrase into the English lexicon and searing the symbolism into the imagination of people who have never read Moby Dick. Hubris, is an overwhelming pride that always, in literature, leads to the destruction to the proud and often to those who are around him or her. Hubris has collateral damage in modern parlance – the entire crew of the *Pequod* in this case save Ishmael. Captain Ahab's overconfidence in his abilities, the technology at his disposal, and the righteousness of his hatred of the beast caused him to ignore all reasonable and rational calls for a new course. Starbuck, Boomer, and others attempted unsuccessfully at various points in the story to dissuade Captain Ahab from his quest. His hubris prevented him from seeing reason and contributed to another main theme of the story.

Obsession

While Captain Ahab is the epitome of overweening hubris, he also is the quintessential example of obsessive hatred. His hatred and his hubris combine to lead to the tragic conclusion of the *Pequod's* voyage. The root of Ahab's obsession is spurred by his irrational hatred of the whale, a refusal to recognize reality coupled with his obsessive embrace of the illusion that he was the sole captain of the destinies of both him and his crew. Ignoring all evidence to the contrary and in defiance of reason and common sense, he insists on leading his crew to their ruin. His single-mindedness and his almost supernatural magnetism lead the crew to either acquiesce, like Starbuck, or to outright give themselves over to the cause – especially after Ahab offers monetary reward to the sailor who spots the whale. Tragic flaws are often excesses of otherwise good traits. Focus on a task or a goal or "eye on the prize" is not a bad thing in and of itself. Ahab personifies the extreme end of that scale, and it kills him and destroys his ship and crew. His innate and learned ability to lead a whaling crew should have been both positive and profitable for crew and owners. Instead his obsession left a literal and figurative wreckage.

Humankind and nature

Another main theme is the idea that humankind is constrained by nature despite scientific and technological progress. The Industrial Revolution is greatly underway, and whale oil is literally fueling the technological progress at the time of the novel's publication. The idea that humans are subject to, as opposed to in control of, nature is a common theme in the 19th century. The crew of the *Pequod*, sailing across the vast oceans and hunting the humongous sperm whales (also called "leviathan") is often and ultimately at the mercy of natural forces: storms, doldrums, heat, and of course the antagonist of the book – Moby Dick. Melville uses *Moby-Dick* to illustrate the point that despite the Biblical mandate to humankind to "subdue" the earth coupled with our growing ability to explain and manipulate nature (looking at all science had accomplished, how to kill whales, etc.), humans are not in sole control, despite the ideals of the Enlightenment, scientific progress, and some evidence to the contrary (Genesis 1:27–28).[6] Additionally, Ahab's enemy is symbolically integrated into his very person. Ahab's earlier conflict with Moby Dick had cost him his leg. Ahab then had a prosthesis fashioned out of whale bone. He was literally and figuratively a combination of human and animal.

Pride and Prejudice by Jane Austen

It is easy for some modern critics to dismiss or minimize Austen as merely an author of light comic novels or novels set in a very specific time and place with a very narrow set of social rules. As to the latter, readers might be correct, but to assume she does not have a more complex view is to miss out on much substance (MacIntyre, 1981, p. 243). *Pride and Prejudice* is no doubt a comedy – filled with ironic wit and pointed observations. But her novels are not "mere" romances or "romantic comedies" as more recent film and television adaptations might lead one to believe. *Pride and Prejudice*, indeed all of Austen's works, are sharp critiques of her society, its rules about marriage and property as well as illustrative of her version of classical virtues as seen through the lens of early 19th century Britain. Philosopher Alasdair MacIntyre (1981) called Jane Austen "the last great representative of the classical tradition of the virtues" (p. 243). Novelist Anthony Trollope (1870/1938, p. 105) said of Jane Austen:

> Miss Austen was surely a great novelist. What she did, she did perfectly. Her work, as far as it goes, is faultless. She wrote of the times in which she lived, of the class of people with which she associated, and in the language which was usual to her as an educated lady. Of romance,—what we generally mean when we speak of romance,—she had no tinge. Heroes and heroines with wonderful adventures there are none in her novels. Of great criminals and hidden crimes she tells us nothing. But she places us in a circle of gentlemen and ladies, and charms us while she tells us with an unconscious accuracy how men should act to women, and women act to men. It is not that her people are all good;—and, certainly, they are not all wise. The faults of some are the anvils on which the virtues of others are hammered till they are bright as steel. In the comedy of folly I know no novelist who has beaten her.

Brief historical context

Jane Austen began writing *Pride and Prejudice* in the mid-1790s and finally published it in 1813. There was great social and political upheaval in England (and in Europe generally) during Austen's lifetime (1775–1817). Great Britain was at war with France from the early 1790s throughout most of Austen's life with a brief respite from 1805 to 1808. Though soldiers were mentioned often in the novel as objects of flirtation for the younger Bennet sisters, Austen alludes nowhere to the British involvement in the continental wars related to Napoleon's visions of French hegemony. The war with Napoleonic France also led to a nearly constant, and not unreasonable, fear of invasion by French forces, especially in southern England until 1805 following the British Navy's defeat of the French Navy at the Battle of Trafalgar. This time period also included The War of 1812 with the United States (Howard, 2003, p. xv). Again, these conflicts are nowhere mentioned, explicitly or implicitly, by Austen. It's not that those conflicts were not important to Miss Austen generally, just that they were not important to her social critique in her novels.

Austen also never dealt with other controversial war-related political issues, such as tax raises on wealthier Britons to pay for the war effort, censorship of perceived sedition, a suspension of the *habeas corpus*,[7] and an outlawing of unofficial contact with France (Fraser, 2003, pp. 482–483). These controversies were at one time or another major issues during the writing of *Pride and Prejudice* yet are nowhere mentioned. In addition to the political upheaval of the day, there was also social upheaval tied to the rapidly changing early-stage Industrial Revolution economy and changes in income distribution. The landed gentry, those who inherited land and lived off the income tied to estates, and those who earned their wealth through work – professions or the merchant class – were coming into increasing contact socially and politically (Howard, 2003). Coupled with this was a change in marriage expectations. The older view of marriages of convenience tied to financial security was giving way to marriage of passion not necessarily connected to social improvement. Austen's works, *Pride and Prejudice* especially, amply illustrate these last two aspects of changing British society (Howard, 2003, p. xx).

Brief biography of Jane Austen

Jane Austen was born in December 1775 as the seventh of eight children to Reverend George and Cassandra Austen. She was not a member of the landed gentry; she both respects and satirizes in many of her novels, but no doubt had contact with many exemplars in her relatively short life. By most accounts she lived a stable, though not completely untroubled, life. Her formal education ended at age 10, but her father had an ample library to which she had access. She accepted one marriage proposal at age 27 and then quickly rescinded it. She never married. *Pride and Prejudice*, her second published novel, was released in 1813. She published three more novels in the next three years. She died at age 41 in 1817. Two other novels were published posthumously (Howard, 2003). Compared to Melville and Cervantes, her relatively short and uneventful life – fully, though not exhaustively, informed by books – yielded no less a formidable wisdom and ability to incisively critique culture and engage readers.

Main Characters

Elizabeth Bennet. Elizabeth is the second-eldest Bennet daughter and the main protagonist. She is a highly intelligent and independent-minded young woman. She has a sharp wit and is an astute judge of people. The story revolves around her initial dislike of Mr. Darcy and her realization of her misreading of his character and actions. She reassesses him and eventually they fall in love.

Fitzwilliam Darcy. He is a wealthy and proud man with impeccable credentials. He falls in love with Elizabeth and reveals a generous, forgiving, and thoughtful nature hidden beneath a stiff and stilted manner. Today Mr. Darcy might be called "socially awkward" despite his high social standing and breeding.

Mr. Bennet. He is Elizabeth's father. His bad choice in marriage coupled with his own apathy have led to his failure to provide a secure financial future for his wife and daughters. Despite his failings, he also provides a voice of reason, especially to Elizabeth.

Mrs. Bennet. Elizabeth's foolish and unrestrained mother who is obsessed with finding husbands for her daughters. The narrator refers to her as "a woman of mean understanding, little information and uncertain temper" (Austen, 1813/2003, p. 7).

Jane Bennet. Jane is the eldest Bennet daughter. She is a kind and well-liked young woman. She is also Elizabeth's confidant and constant support. She and Bingley are in love, but both are cautious about revealing the depth of their feelings.

Lydia Bennet. She is youngest daughter of five. Her gross immaturity and recklessness, evidenced by running away with Wickham, almost ruins the family.

Charles Bingley. Bingley is a wealthy man and close friend of Mr. Darcy. He falls in love with Jane and while he is a man of good character he is easily influenced by others, especially Mr. Darcy.

George Wickham. A handsome and personal military officer and scoundrel in whom Elizabeth is initially interested. He eventually runs off with and is forced to marry Lydia.

Lady Catherine De Bourgh. She is Mr. Darcy's overbearing, meddlesome, and arrogant aunt, and she consistently dominates Mr. Collins. She assumes that Mr. Darcy will marry her daughter.

Mr. Collins. He is Mr. Bennet's cousin, who will inherit Longbourn, the Bennet's home, after Mr. Bennet's death. Following Lady Catherine De Bourgh's demand, he seeks a bride, first proposing to Elizabeth – who rejects his offer – then to Charlotte Lucas, Elizabeth's close friend.

Charlotte Lucas. She is Elizabeth's close friend and confidant, who disappoints Elizabeth by marrying Mr. Collins for "convenience" – money and security.

Synopsis

The Bennet family has five unmarried daughters. Jane is the oldest, Elizabeth is the second, and Lydia is the youngest. These three play the major roles in the story. Marriage is a very important aspect of social life in the Great Britain of the novel, especially for the Bennets, whose father has failed to adequately set up his daughters financially. They will be reliant on "good marriages" (not merely love but wealth, property, and title) to be taken care of upon Mr. Bennet's death. A young, wealthy, and single gentleman named Bingley rents a manor, Netherfield, near the Bennets' home village of Longbourn. His wealth, class, and availability send the village into a frenzy of activity and excitement, especially in Mrs. Bennet.

Mr. Bennet calls on Mr. Bingley in an attempt to make a connection for Jane, his oldest daughter. Following that, the Bennets attend a ball at which Mr. Bingley is present. He is smitten with Jane spending much of the evening dancing and talking with her. His close and also unmarried friend, Mr. Darcy, is less friendly, haughtily refusing to dance with Elizabeth. His demeanor makes most people see him as arrogant and obnoxious.

As the story progresses through many other balls and other social gatherings, Mr. Darcy becomes increasingly attracted to Elizabeth's charm, wit, and intelligence. Jane's friendship with Mr. Bingley also continues to grow. While walking to Bingley's house Jane gets ill after being caught in a heavy rain, forcing her to stay at Netherfield for several days. In order to tend to Jane, Elizabeth hikes across muddy fields and arrives with a filthy dress, much to the disdain of the condescending Miss Bingley, Charles Bingley's sister. Miss Bingley's boorish behavior grows out of jealousy as she notices Mr. Darcy, whom she is pursuing, pays much attention to Elizabeth.

Elizabeth and Jane return home after Jane's recovery and find Mr. Collins visiting their household. Mr. Collins is a young clergyman and is the heir to Mr. Bennet's property, under the British common law concept of entailment.[8] This produces a conundrum for the sonless Bennet family and the five daughters for whom Mr. Bennet has failed to provide upon his death. Mr. Collins is obsequious and pompous. That being said, he is also unmarried, has the right to the Bennet property, and is quite taken with the Bennet girls generally and Elizabeth in particular. Shortly after his arrival, he makes a proposal of marriage to Elizabeth. She turns him down gently. Recovering quickly, Collins soon after becomes engaged to Elizabeth's close companion Charlotte Lucas. Lucas is the daughter of landed gentry who has little in the way of resources other than a title. Charlotte needs the marriage for financial security, and they are soon married. Meanwhile, the youngest three Bennet girls, Lydia especially, have become friendly with militia officers stationed in a nearby town. George Wickham, a handsome young soldier is one of them. He is also friendly toward Elizabeth and tells her a long story accusing Mr. Darcy of mistreating him and cheating him out of his inheritance.

At the beginning of winter, the Bingleys and Mr. Darcy return to London. Later that winter, Jane visits friends in London also hoping to see Mr. Bingley and continue their friendship and possible courtship. Instead she sees Miss Bingley who is rude to her. Mr. Bingley does not visit her at all over her time in London even though they had gotten along well at Longbourn. The marriage prospects for the Bennet girls, especially Jane at this point, seem to be dwindling.

That spring, Elizabeth stays with Charlotte, who now lives near the home of Mr. Collins's patron, Lady Catherine de Bourgh. She is also Mr. Darcy's aunt. Mr. Darcy calls on Lady Catherine and encounters Elizabeth, causing him to make numerous visits to the Collins's home. One day, he professes his love for Elizabeth and offers a surprising proposal of marriage. Elizabeth, taken aback and influenced by Wickham's stories of a cruel and mean Mr. Darcy, quickly and firmly refuses. She rebukes Mr. Darcy frankly telling him she thinks him arrogant and unpleasant. She also excoriates him for influencing Bingley away from Jane and disinheriting Wickham. The next day Mr. Darcy gives Elizabeth a letter in which puts a better light on his actions. He admits convincing Bingley to distance himself from Jane, because he thought she was not serious about him. As for Wickham, Mr. Darcy tells Elizabeth that he is a liar and that the real cause of their disagreement was Wickham's attempt to elope with his young sister.

The letter causes Elizabeth to reevaluate both Mr. Darcy and Wickham. The militia, Wickham included, is leaving town making the youngest Bennet girls distraught. Lydia manages to obtain permission from her father to spend the summer with a family friend in Brighton, where Wickham's regiment will be stationed. Elizabeth goes on a journey with the Gardiners − her uncle and aunt. The trip takes her to the North and eventually to the neighborhood of Pemberley, Mr. Darcy's estate. She visits Pemberley, after making sure that Mr. Darcy is away, and enjoys the building and grounds, all the while hearing from his servants how wonderful, generous he is. Mr. Darcy suddenly arrives and behaves cordially toward her. Remaining silent about his proposal, he generously entertains the Gardiners and also invites Elizabeth to meet his sister.

Soon thereafter, word reaches Elizabeth that her youngest sister Lydia and Wickham have eloped and that the couple is missing, suggesting that they may be living together out of wedlock. Such a situation would bring shame and humiliation on the entire family. Mr. Bennet and Mr. Gardiner go off in search of them. Mr. Bennet eventually returns home empty-handed. A bit later, Mr. Gardiner finds the couple and informs the Bennets that Wickham has agreed to marry Lydia in exchange for an annual income. The Bennets assume that Mr. Gardiner paid Wickham, but Elizabeth learns that the source of the money was really Mr. Darcy.

Wickham and Lydia return to Longbourn briefly before departing for Wickham's new military posting in northern England. Bingley returns to Netherfield and resumes his courtship of Jane. Mr. Darcy comes with him and visits the Bennets. Bingley proposes to Jane, to the horror of his haughty sister, but to the delight and relief of Jane's family. While the family celebrates, Lady Catherine de Bourgh pays a visit. She confronts Elizabeth saying she has heard that Mr. Darcy is planning to marry her. Judging Elizabeth to be an unsuitable match for her nephew, she demands that Elizabeth promise to refuse him. Elizabeth pointedly rejects this demand, reserving the right to choose her own course in life. Soon after, Elizabeth and Mr. Darcy go out walking when he tells her that his feelings have not altered since the spring and his first proposal. Elizabeth, in a culmination of self-realization about her own pride and her love of Mr. Darcy accepts his proposal. The novel ends shortly after the marriages of Jane and Elizabeth.

Main themes

Pride and Prejudice

Pride and Prejudice is about many things: social class, relationships between men and women, the danger of jumping to conclusions, self-knowledge, and courtship and marriage. Couched in a "comedy of manners,"[9] two of its overarching themes, as the reader can readily surmise from the title, are pride and prejudice. The excess or lack of either of these traits can cause problems leading to potentially dire consequences. Indeed, many scholars see Austen advocating for a class of traits called "virtues," the possession and exercise of which – in the proper balance – contribute to living "the good life" or "human flourishing" (Toner, 2017). Good character keeps the traits of pride and prejudice in check. As Mr. Darcy notes in an early conversation with Elizabeth, ". . . it has been the study of my life to avoid those weakness which often expose a strong understanding to ridicule" (Austen, 1813/2003, p. 57). Elizabeth teases him that he "has no defect" to which Mr. Darcy demurs that of course he has faults (Austen, 1813/2003, p. 57). This early conversation reveals an excess of pride in both characters: Mr. Darcy's pride comes from on "high" toward the lower social classes and Elizabeth's comes from "down low" – toward the upper classes. One may be socially superior or inferior in a given society, but any person can feel superior to another person. Pride, in this instance, fuels prejudice.

Austen also portrays these virtues in the various excesses and deficiencies of a multitude of her characters and especially in the growth of her two lead characters: Elizabeth and Mr. Darcy. Both characters display the deficiencies of pride and prejudice as well as the proper balance of pride. "Prejudice" here does not imply the more modern implications of that term where unlawful or immoral racial, gender, religious, or other bias is usually implicit, if not explicit. To be sure, prejudice is portrayed as a negative trait by Austen, especially in Mr. Darcy's disdain for the *noveau riche*[10] professionals who do not have the manners and values of the aristocratic landed gentry. This criticism is also seen in Elizabeth's prejudgment of Mr. Darcy as cruel and mean as she credulously believes Wickham's story as opposed to taking more time to find further evidence or even asking Mr. Darcy himself about the events. The inability to control pride and to focus it correctly leads to prejudice which almost keeps the protagonists from ever realizing the "good" marriage they both wanted.

Marriage and family

Austen also uses this novel to highlight marriage and family and the importance of a good marriage as well as good decision making in general when it comes to family. MacIntyre (1981) calls Austen's novels

> a moral criticism of parents and guardians quite as much as of young romantics; for the worst parents and guardians – the silly Mrs. Bennet and the irresponsible Mr. Bennet, for example – are what the romantic young may become if they do not learn what they ought to learn on the way to being married.
>
> (p. 239)

Pride and Prejudice relatedly serves as a criticism of the economic realities of the time. These realities make a good marriage – "good" measured as much, if not more, by financial security and social status than by romantic passion and emotion – of outsized importance. This importance leads, in different ways, Elizabeth's good friend Charlotte Lucas and the youngest Bennet daughter Lydia to make poor marriage choices, albeit in different ways and for different reasons. Indeed the lack of character or the right kind of pride affects the very marriage of Elizabeth's parents. Judicious pride in one's own family and in one's own self can help one avoid making foolish marriage choices which have lifelong consequences.

Commenting upon her parents' marriage, following a scene where Elizabeth pleads with her father to prevent Lydia from following the troops to their new base (Austen, 1813/2003, pp. 227–228), the narrator noted that Mr. Bennet had married Mrs. Bennet based on her "youth and beauty" (p. 231) and that her vapidity had basically ended any real affection. He was not the sort to resort to adultery or other indiscretions but is reduced to appreciating his wife for the amusement her "ignorance and folly" provided (p. 231). But his lack of respect did have negative consequences.

The narrator noted,

> Elizabeth, however, had never been blind to the impropriety of her father's behaviour as a husband. She had always seen it with pain; but respecting his abilities, and grateful for his affectionate treatment of herself, she endeavored to forget what she could not overlook, and to banish from her thoughts that continual breach of conjugal obligation and decorum, which, in exposing his wife to the contempt of her own children, was so highly reprehensible. But she had never felt so strongly as now the disadvantages which must attend the children of so unsuitable a marriage, not even so fully aware of the evils arising from so ill-judged a direction of talents – talents which, rightly used, might at least have preserved the respectability of his daughters, even if incapable of enlarging the mind of his wife.
>
> (Austen, 1813/2003, pp. 231–232)

Self-discovery

Additionally, the theme includes the capacity for self-discovery and to make changes based on new found awarenesses. "Self" discovery is a bit of a misnomer as most such discoveries are prompted by circumstances or interactions with others. As a result of Mr. Darcy's long letter, Elizabeth reevaluated her pride in her own ability to judge character and realized her prejudice toward Mr. Darcy was based on circumstantial, which is to say incomplete, evidence. She confessed:

> How despicably have I acted!" she cried. "I who have prided myself on my discernment! I, who have valued myself on my abilities! Who have often disdained the generous candour of my sister [Jane], and gratified my vanity in useless or blameable distrust. How humiliating is this discovery! Yet, how just a humiliation! Had I been in love, I could not have been more wretchedly blind. But vanity, not love, has been my folly. Pleased with the preference of one, and offended by the neglect of the other, on the very beginning of our acquaintance, I have courted prepossession and ignorance, and driven reason away where either were concerned. Till this moment I never knew myself.
>
> (Austen, 1813/2003, pp. 204–205)

Likewise, Mr. Darcy, as all good protagonists – and similar to Elizabeth, had his own personal epiphany. Elizabeth's misinformed, but effective, dressing down of Mr. Darcy triggered his. Following their engagement and during a conversation where they clear the air Mr. Darcy told Elizabeth,

> The recollection of what I then said, of my conduct, my manners, my expressions during the whole of it, is now, and has been many months, inexpressible painful to me. Your reproof, so well applied, I shall never forget: 'Had you behaved in a more gentleman-like manner.' Those were your words. You know not, can scarcely conceive, how they have tortured me; though it was some time, I confess, before I was reasonable enough to allow their justice.
>
> (Austen, 1813/2003, p. 355)

Their respective epiphanies resulted in their own self-improvement. Discovering a flaw does little good, however, if it is not repaired. Well-written; well-rounded protagonists, like Elizabeth Bennet and Mr. Darcy, set about fixing their discovered flaws. The protagonists put to use their discoveries by realizing each other's virtue, reconciling, and then forgiving each other's weaknesses while promising to limit, if not eliminate, their own excessive pride.

Summary and conclusion

Don Quixote, Moby-Dick, and Pride and Prejudice have all been celebrated for decades and centuries for their treatment of universal themes, fully developed characters, and skillfully written plots. They are often, if not universally, recognized as among the greatest works of narrative fiction from the past five centuries.

The examples of haughty pride, destructive obsession, or quixotic pursuits have inspired generations of people from all walks of life and a wide variety of cultural experiences to adopt or avoid those very traits in themselves or others. People do not have to experience life aboard a 19th century whaling ship to recognize the Captain Ahabs that sometimes enter their lives at work or at school or wherever a hubristic and obsessive leader arises. *Moby-Dick*, then, is not merely a "whale tale" but is something much deeper and longer lasting. Its impact and truthfulness transcend its specific setting and time. It is a great novel that deserves reading by people going forward not just for the ripping good yarn but for the deeper meanings it has to offer the layperson or the professional.

The foregoing examples are just a small sample of the themes, characters, and plots great novels provide. This chapter is hardly exhaustive on even these three works not to mention the myriad of other great novels. Readers generally, and as will be shown in the following chapter, leaders and followers, have much to glean from reading these three works and great novels more broadly. As has been shown, a compelling narrative following a tried and true plotline and skillfully communicated can help convey ideals, goals, and virtues. Great novels serve as a repository of ideas for framing an organizational narrative and of plots that can be analogized for stories as leaders attempt to shape and motivate followers to reach a goal. Great literature also provides templates and clues for leaders and followers to identify possible character types. Captain Ahabs are not the only characters that novels convey. Elizabeth Bennet may arrive in organizations – quick witted, relatively inexperienced but well-meaning and sharp. *Pride and Prejudice* provides insight into how to deal with or motivate such a character in a leader's organization. It can also help a follower who has a leader resembling any number of characters in any given novel, on how to interact or perhaps even prepare for eventualities.

Additionally, every story needs a protagonist – a hero or well-meaning and persistent or hard-working individual who persists in the quest or overcomes the conflict or tension in any given story. Novels provide guidance in how to overcome a variety of antagonists, whether natural, other people, or events that are outside of the control of the main protagonist. Again, *Pride and Prejudice* here as well as *Don Quixote* can help. In both novels, it can be argued that each main protagonist, Mr. Darcy, Elizabeth Bennet and Don Quixote, is also his or her own antagonist. In the words of American comic artist Walt Kelly's *Pogo* "We have met the enemy and he is us" (Kelly, 1970). In other words, people are often their own worst enemies or their own antagonists. Darcy and Elizabeth's excessive pride and prejudice nearly torpedoes their romance before it even has a chance to really take root and blossom. The ability to discover and realize their own failings returns them to being protagonists in their own stories. Likewise, Don Quixote, in his lengthy quest is in many ways his own worst enemy as he fails or refuses to recognize the reality of any given situation. As novels can be a tool of self-discovery and emotional intelligence, it is important for potential and current leaders to recognize when they are their own antagonists.

The novels also provide readers with insights on what makes for a good narrative, not just for novels, but for leading and managing organizations. Chapter 4 demonstrates that leaders and managers who engage in good storytelling, who shape the workplace narratives on par with what makes for good literature, create an esprit de corps among stakeholders not found when lesser quality narratives are in place. Leaders and managers are the protagonists for their organizations. They shape the plot and narrate the story to help others makes sense of the organizations.

Notes

1 The Council of Trent (1545–1563), prompted by the Protestant Reformation, required all books in the Roman Catholic realm to be examined and approved for publication. Authors and printers who filed to get prior approval of publication could be assessed a fee or suffer excommunication from the Church.

2 While Don Quixote is the protagonist of the story, the heroes are the malevolent friends and benevolent strangers in the story who come from all walks of life.

3 Don Quixote is speaking to his squire as Sancho embarks on his new role as governor of the Isle of Barataria.

4 The *Essex* was a whaling ship sunk by a sperm whale that rammed it twice. The surviving crew then suffered a long spell of being castaways on a deserted island as well as stories of cannibalism. The story is credited as being the inspiration for *Moby-Dick* and was most recently portrayed in Nathaniel Philbrick's book *In the Heart of the Sea*, Viking Press (2000), and a 2015 feature film based on the book directed by Ron Howard.

5 The story of Jonah, from the Old Testament "Book of Jonah" involves an Israelite prophet (Jonah) ordered by God to deliver a judgment against the city of Nineveh in Mesopotamia. Jonah, out of a mixture of ethnic hatred and fear attempts to run away. He boards a ship headed the opposite way across the Mediterranean Sea. God sends a storm to distress the ship and the sailors are afraid of impending death. Jonah knows God has sent the storm due to his disobedience and he convinces the crew to throw him overboard and the storm will calm. They obey, the storm ceases and God sends a "big fish" – often called a whale – to swallow Jonah up. Jonah spends a few days in the belly of the beast and the beast spits Jonah out on the beach and Jonah then heads to Nineveh to deliver the message God had demanded. Needless to say, in addition to the theological lessons in the story of "Jonah and the whale," it holds an important place in the lore and superstitions of mariners.

6 Genesis 1:27–28 (New American Standard.)

> 27 God created man in His own image, in the image of God He created him; male and female He created them. 28 God blessed them; and God said to them, 'Be fruitful and multiply, and fill the earth, and subdue it; and rule over the fish of the sea and over the birds of the sky and over every living thing that moves on the earth.'

This concept was widely known and believed in Melville's time and was also coming under attack with the ideas published by Charles Darwin and others not a decade after the publication of *Moby-Dick* in 1851.

7 *Habeas Corpus* refers, broadly, to the right of citizens to be informed of charges filed against them and protects against unjust imprisonment. It is seen, both in the U.S. and the U.K. as a fundamental right that is only limited in extreme circumstances, and even then rarely.

8   Merriam-Webster's Dictionary of Law (2011) defines "entail" thusly: "as to make (an estate in real property) a fee tail: limit the descent of (real property) by restricting inheritance to specific descendants who cannot convey or transfer the property." Mr. Collins was made the specific heir to the Bennet estate. A Bennet son would have been the superior heir to the estate and thus would be the one to provide for his sisters and mother upon the death of Mr. Bennet and in the event the daughters failed to make a good marriage. This is an underlying tension to the plot.

9   A comedy of manners is a genre of fiction that satirizes social class and the mores and manners of the time in which the story is set.

10   One of the tensions in the novel is landed gentry, represented by men with titles who inherit land like Mr Darcy, Mr. Bennet, et al., and men whose money comes through professions like law. These "new money" folk are not usually as cultured or sophisticated according to the likes of Darcy.

References

Armstrong, P. (2004). "Leviathan is a skein of networks": Translations of nature and culture in Moby-Dick. *ELH, 71*(4), 1039–1063.

Austen, J. (1813/2003). *Pride and prejudice.* New York, NY: Barnes & Noble Classics.

Bloom, H. (1994/2014). *The western canon: The books and school of the ages.* Retrieved from https://ebookcentral.proquest.com

Brooks, V. Wyck. (1915). *America's coming of age.* Boston, MA: E. P. Dutton and Co.

Caponegro, M. (2008). The translator. *Conjunctions, 50,* 403–414.

Cervantes Saavedra, M. de. (1604/1956). Don Quixote (J. Cohen, Trans.) Baltimore, MD: Penguin Books.

Chrisafis, A. (2002, May 8). Don Quixote is the world's best book say the world's top authors. *The Guardian.*

Fraser, R. (2003). *The story of Britain.* New York, NY: W.W. Norton and Company.

Gander, C. (2010). Muriel Rukeyser, America, and the "Melville Revival." *Journal of American Studies, 44*(4), 759–775.

Greenberg, M (2004). In search of Don Quixote. *New Criterion, 23*(2), pp. 28–34.

Hart, T. R. (2009). What's Funny about Don Quixote? *Hispanic Research Journal: Iberian and Latin American Studies, 10*(3), 227–232.

Howard, C. (2003). Introduction. In Jane Austen (Ed.), *Pride and prejudice* (pp. xiii–xxxv). New York, NY: Barnes & Noble Classics.

Howard, L. (1950). *Herman Melville: A biography.* Berkeley: University of California Press.

Ife, B. (2002). *The historical and social context.* Cambridge, UK: Cambridge University Press.

Kelly, W. (1970). *Earth Day Poster.*

Layson, H., & Carman, G. (2013, November 24). *The world of Don Quixote: Digital collections for the classroom.* Retrieved January 30, 2019, from https://dcc.newberry.org/collections/the-world-of-don-quixote

MacIntyre, A. C. (1981). *After virtue: A study in moral theory* (2nd ed.). Notre Dame, IN: University of Notre Dame Press.

McCrory, D. (2014). *No ordinary man: The life and times of Miguel de Cervantes*. Mineola, NY: Dover Publications.

Napierkowski, M., & Stanley, D. (2000). *Novels for students: Presenting analysis, context, and criticism on commonly studied novels*. Farmington Hills, MI: Gale Group.

Ormsby, J. (1855). Introduction. In M. Cervantes Saavedra (Ed.), *The ingenious gentleman of Don Quixote of La Mancha* (pp. 1–80). New York: Farrar, Straus, Giroux.

Paretsky, S. (1999). Damned by dollars. *American Scholar, 68*(1), 160.

Parker, H. (1996). *Herman Melville: A biography (Volume 1, 1819–1851)*. Baltimore, MD: The John Hopkins University Press.

Renker, E. (2014). *Introduction to Moby Dick by Herman Melville*. New York, NY: Signet Classics.

Seymour-Smith, M. (1998). *The 100 most influential books ever written: The history of thought from ancient times to today*. New York, NY: Barnes & Noble Books.

Shaw, B. (1903). *Maxims for revolutionists*. Retrieved from http://archive.org/details/maximsforrevolut26107gut

Shoemaker, N. (2013). Mr. Tashtego: Native American whalemen in Antebellum New England. *Journal of the Early Republic, 33*(1), 109–132.

Stavans, I. (2005). Don Quixote at 400: Still Conquering Hearts. *Chronicle of Higher Education, 51*(18), B11.

Toner, C. (2017). Jane Austen on practical wisdom, constancy, and unreserve. *Philosophy and Literature, 41*(1A), 178–194. https://doi.org/10.1353/phl.2017.0029

Trilling, L. (1953). *The liberal imagination: Essays on literature and society*. Garden City, NY: Doubleday.

Trollope, A. (1870/1938). *Four lectures* (Parrish, M., ed.) London, England: Constable.

Wardropper, B. W. (1965). "Don Quixote": Story or history? *Modern Philology, 63*(1), 1–11.

3 Leadership insights from *Don Quixote*, *Moby-Dick*, and *Pride and Prejudice*

Miguel de Cervantes, Herman Melville, and Jane Austen crafted exemplary narratives with nuanced themes, plots, and characters that provide to this day insightful lessons for living and leading well. This chapter evaluates several themes from each novel and makes explicit and visceral connections to the leadership and management research, illustrating how the study of great literature can tutor and mentor readers to be aesthetically appealing and engaging leaders.

Seven leadership and management lessons from Cervantes's *Don Quixote*

"Don Quixote effect"

The Don Quixote effect involves two elements. The first is that people become what they read and watch. For practical purposes, the mind is somewhat of a *tabula rasa*. Steven Sample (2001), former president of the University of Southern California, in his book, *The Contrarian's Guide to Leadership*, noted that "to a greater extent than we realize, and to a far greater extent than we ever care to admit, we are what we read" (p. 55). Because of this, Sample encouraged leaders to read the supertexts of civilization. Sample astutely observed that:

> A leader's choices of vocabulary [quixotic], metaphors [tilting at windmills], syntax, phraseology [proverbial sayings] and patterns of speech are all affected to a greater or lesser extent by the supertexts, because the leader knows (or unconsciously senses) that the language of these texts (updated with a bit of current jargon) has a high probability of resonating with his followers.

> (p. 59)

It is by reading numerous books about chivalry that Don Quixote decided to become a knight-errant. Cervantes (1604/1998) illustrated that one's thought life shapes his or her imagination and behavior.

> He [Don Quixote] had filled his imagination with everything that he had read, with enchantments, knightly encounters, battles, challenges, wounds, with tales of love and its torments, and all sorts of impossible things, and as a result had come to believe that all these fictitious happenings were true; they were more real to him than anything else in the world.
>
> (Cervantes, 1604/1998, p. 27)

Throughout the novel, Don Quixote repeatedly cited the stories of chivalry from his obsessive readings to make sense of his adventures and misadventures. While it may be easy to dismiss Don Quixote as a lunatic, the point is that what people say and do is largely derived from the thoughts informing their schema (context specific frames of reference) and worldview (more generalized beliefs and assumptions about the nature of reality and values), demonstrating what Sample (2001) observed – people talk and act like what they read.

Basically, people draw from their knowledge to contextualize their experiences and "enact" their environments. Personal schematas "help people simplify, effectively manage, and make sense of information in their surrounding environments and guide the cognition, interpretation, and ways of understanding events or objects" (Chung-Ming & Woodman, 1995, p. 538). Schemas are a subset of one's worldview. Every individual has his or her own schema about leadership and followership and a worldview about what is ultimately true that guides how he or she responds to and engages the world and conducts his or her leadership practices. In essence, as a person "thinks within himself, so he is" (Proverbs 23:7 New American Standard).

The second element of the Don Quixote effect is axiomatic to the first. Exposure to certain "feel good" stories prompts "a temporary cognitive and emotional assumption of idealism" (Shapiro & Rucker, 2004, p. 448). People inherit a sense of altruism and hope when exposed to inspirational and noble stories. Exposure to virtuous ideas and behavior inspires both good feelings and good behavior. Ariely (2013) documented that when moral examples and reminders are present, people tend to make moral decisions. Heroic stories socialize people to be the protagonists of their own story.

Don Quixote illustrates that people think and act consistently with the ideas they absorb and that good thoughts and actions inspire others to good thoughts and actions. Leaders should cultivate proper insights, use of language, and passions by reading judiciously and frequently.

Quixotic ambitions

Leaders are expected to be visionary people. Ryan (2009) observed in his *Forbes* article, *Leadership Success Always Starts with Vision,* that one of the few fundamentals that makes great leaders effective is a compelling vision. Leaders have to lead somewhere, and truly exemplary leaders have compelling and inspiring destinations in mind (Kouzes & Posner, 2012). Because visionary leaders tend to see the future differently, they are often too easily viewed as crazy, at least initially. For example, Howard Schultz created Starbucks by selling a social experience around a $4.00 cup of coffee. At the same time, a lack of outrageous vision creates missed opportunities.

Visionary leaders tasked with creating new futures often clash with successful managers tasked to maintain organizational stability (Kotter, 1990). Visionary leaders often end up being cast as heroes or fools. They create disruptive change, making them vulnerable to pejorative labels. When at-one-time crazy sounding ideas come to fruition, the previously labeled "crazy person" is considered a genius.

George Bernard Shaw (1903) quipped in his *Maxims for Revolutionists* "that reasonable man adapts himself to the world: the unreasonable one persists in trying to adapt the world to himself. Therefore all progress depends on the unreasonable man" (p. 238).[1] De Unamuno (1925) astutely observed that "to attain the impossible, one must attempt the absurd" (p. 104). Unamuno and Shaw recognized that one needs to be a little unreasonable and crazy if he or she is going to change the world. The challenge is discerning the difference between leaders who risk pursuing good ideas with some probability of success from those ideas that have no probability of success. *Don Quixote* provides a language for a conversation about that space between heroic and foolish actions.

Cervantes (1604/1998) ushered the adjective *"quixotic"* and the metaphor *"tilting at windmills"* into the international lexicon forever providing a language to discern when innovative ideas are crazy enough to possibly work or too crazy to ever work. Quixotic is now a term of endearment for that space. Being quixotic gives people permission to think and act nobly outside of the box without being labeled eccentric or crazy and legitimizes the space in risky endeavors when a leader will either emerge a hero or a fool. The term gives grace for benevolent leaders to appear foolish for a while. The term also emboldens leaders to take impressive risks and change reality for the better.

Cervantes (1604/1998) suggested that good leaders need to be a bit quixotic in their pursuits. The Spanish philosopher Miguel de Unamuno went a step further in his musings on the philosophy of Don Quixote, calling for leaders and managers to be heroes and, in doing so, like the *Man of La*

Mancha, to be a bit ridiculous relative to the status quo. De Unamuno (1954) stated that "The greatest height of heroism to which an individual, like a people, can attain is to know how to face ridicule; better still, to how to make oneself ridiculous and not to shrink from ridicule" (p. 315).

Persistence

In addition to enduring ridicule for pursuing quixotic ambitions, leaders experience hardships, headaches, and heartaches. Leaders are also frequently misunderstood, misquoted, and misrepresented. Axiomatic to being a quixotic leader is persistence. Don Quixote demonstrated that while virtuous leadership is rewarding, it is not for the fainthearted. In a conversation with his niece, who was trying to talk sense in to her uncle, Don Quixote was cognizant that he was taking the path less traveled when he shared,

> Knowing as I do all the innumerable hardships that go with knight-errantry, I also know the infinite number of good things that are to be attained by it. I am aware that the path of virtue is a straight and narrow one.
>
> (Cervantes, 1604/1998, p. 642)

Ryan (2009) noted that while leadership success starts with a compelling vision, it is persistence that brings visions to fruition. Ryan described five keys to successful and sustained leadership. He provided insights to leadership that align with the leadership lessons from *Don Quixote* – Principles, Passion, People, Performance, and Persistence. No doubt that Don Quixote was driven by chivalric principles and a passion. While his performance as a knight was laughable, Don Quixote remained undaunted by the number of intense setbacks from one misadventure to the next. Persistence is the foundational quality for successful leadership because every leader experiences setbacks and losses. According to Ryan, successful leaders double-down their resolve and move forward, in part driven by their passions and principles.

The biographies of great business and political leaders like Thomas Edison, Henry Ford, Sam Walton, Steve Jobs, Abraham Lincoln, Gandhi, and Martin Luther King Jr. reveal that their celebrated accomplishments were forged on the anvils of repeated failures and hardships that would have deterred lesser people who lacked the resolve or grit to keep going. Grit is a relatively new concept to the field of leadership studies. Duckworth (2016) documented that passions combined with long-term perseverance, not genius, drive success. She evaluated what caused people to complete arduous challenges when others bailed out and noticed something that she referred to as grit. She described grit as "having a passion to accomplish a particular top-level goal *and* the perseverance to follow through" (p. 250). Grit is the determinative factor to success. The good news according to Duckworth, people can parent, coach, and lead for grit in supportive situations with high expectations. Duckworth even stated, "If you're a leader, and you want the people in your organization to be grittier, create a gritty culture" (p. 245).

Passions without persistence or grit are day dreams. Persistence or grit without passion is slavery. *Don Quixote* reinforced that grit is a co-requisite to quixotic ambitions. Whether Don Quixote's virtue made him mad or his madness made him virtuous, leaders learn that if Don Quixote can persist and survive hardship and hurt in his noble and imagined quixotic pursuits, so can they in their worthy pursuits.

Benevolent friends and strangers

When evaluating his social standing as a person from a relatively humble family pedigree, Don Quixote observed that people's destiny and success were dependent on their choices, not their position at birth.

> . . . all the people in this world may be divided into four classes: those who from humble beginnings have grown and expanded until they have attained a pinnacle of greatness; those who were great to begin with and who have since consistently maintained their original state; those who have arrived at a pyramidal point, having progressively diminished and consumed the greatness that was theirs at the start until, like the point of the pyramid with respect to its base or foundation, they have come to be nothing at all; and, finally, there is the vast majority who had neither a good start nor a subsequent history that was in any way out of the ordinary and who accordingly will have a nameless end, like the ordinary plebeian stock.
>
> (Cervantes, 1604/1998, p. 640)

According to Cervantes (1604/1998), while most people will have nameless endings, they can have heroic presents. The real hero of the story, arguably, is not Don Quixote, but Sancho Panza. Visionary leaders need followers and friends who keep them grounded, help them advance their causes, and intervene when things go awry. Kellerman (2008), in her book, *Followership*, astutely acknowledged that followers are equally as important as leaders, and that leadership only happens when followers allow it. Cervantes demonstrated that the acts of kindness from both benevolent and malevolent friends and strangers are critical to Don Quixote's survival and society in general. The curator, priest, Sancho, innkeepers, shepherds, and fellow travelers serve as what Shoup (2005) identified as prodigious patrons.

> Prodigious patrons are people who, almost with a providential timing, and unwittingly at the time, become strategic catalysts for the leader to make it to the next plateau of success or downfall. Throughout the leader's career, there was a steady stream or supply of advisors, financial backers, encouragers, kind strangers, and colleagues so that without such involvement, the leader's story may well have had a different outcome. What set the exemplary leaders apart in this area from the competent leaders was the nature of the advisors. Repeatedly the exemplary leaders cited a "moral voice," the "nudging moral elbow," or a "surrogate moral conscience" of some significant other guiding their thinking.
>
> The "prodigious patrons" serve a substantive or monumental role in shaping and maintaining a leader's success and influence. The term "prodigious" is used because it means monumental or consequential effect or outcome from a particular influence at a particular time. Prodigious also has the connotation of providence and fate, reflecting that timing of the influence was an essential factor in the eventual outcome. The prodigious people played such a role that, one is left to wonder, if that person had not acted when he or she did in the manner he or she did, the outcome of the specific sequence of events would have been significantly altered.
>
> (pp. 41–42)

Cervantes relayed many heroic stories of those who encountered Don Quixote demonstrating that one does not need a title of nobility to do noble things and that individual successes are predicated on the numerous good acts of tertiary characters. Leaders and managers would do well to develop strong networks and teams to leverage the power of the collective.

Critical commentary

Cervantes provided extensive cultural context to Don Quixote's adventures and misadventures and imbued stories with historical details. The novel included critical commentary on the times when religious and political expressions were under strict control from the Roman Catholic Church and the State. Don Quixote's madness gave Cervantes cover to challenge the status quo and insulated him from religious or legal sanctions.

Byrne (2012), in *Law and History in Cervantes' Don Quixote*, provided a detailed comparison of Cervantes's novel with contemporary religious and legal practices:

> History as a perceptive commentary and justice as thematic content are two key elements of Miguel de Cervantes' *Don Quixote*, as evidenced in the author's multiple references to the contentious literary debates of his day, his use of formal and thematic aspects of contemporary historiographical questions, and his protagonist's exploration of the meaning of justice.
>
> (p. 6)

Byrne documented how "Cervantes saturates *Don Quixote* with juridical material, from the multiple law-breaking characters to their copious commentary on the meaning of right and wrong" (p. 44) and that:

> Don Quixote and Sancho Panza personify the debate on history and jurisprudence, and elucidate how historical law both can and cannot be applied in a contemporary context. Cervantes makes it specific to Spain's own legal codes and history while offering a humanist, inclusive, yet discriminating eye for philosophical detail as part of the whole picture.
>
> (p. 20)

Cervantes used plays on words and numerous events to highlight various issues and in this role served as a critical commentator on society. In terms of law and politics, Cervantes, as noted earlier, was personally well acquainted with the vagaries of Spain's legal system and its plethora of statutes, regulations, and orders. In one episode, after Sancho Panza is declared "Governor" of his own Isle of Barataria, a doctor takes it upon himself to direct what Sancho may or may not eat. There was a move afoot in late 16th-century Spain for the government to appoint physicians to dictate what the people could and could not eat and the quantity of such food. Sancho balked at such control, threatens the doctor with physical violence, and removed him from Court. Sancho Panza's disdain for such control reflected a common sense resistance to intrusive control. The episode is so ridiculous that even this thinly veiled satire of a specific contemporary issue passed the censor in 1615.

In addition, Cervantes seems to be commenting on the amount of laws and the impossibility of keeping all of the laws. In the modern age, this concept is often referred to as "overcriminalization" – the criminalizing of conduct, which then makes it almost impossible to fully obey the law. Byrne

(2012) cited that in Cervantes's Spain, as in traditional English Common Law systems, "ignorance of the law is no excuse" (p. 83). Even rubes such as Sancho Panza were held responsible for knowing all of the law – regardless of how much law there was. The proliferation of legal codes – especially to the point that those charged with knowledge cannot, in fact, know all the law, much less keep it – brings into question the wisdom of the lawgivers. Is the point of the law to maintain public order and stability or to entrap well-meaning, but sometimes licentious citizens or subjects?

Byrne (2012) noted that, "it is evident that almost all the characters in *Don Quixote* . . . are breaking one law or another" (p. 101) Cervantes used many examples of arcane laws in his narrative. The examples include such mundane deeds as women wearing veils, religious men wearing nightshirts outdoors at night, and using more than 12 torches or wax candles in a burial ritual to many of the characters who violate various Spanish "sumptuary laws" by wearing too many of the wrong types of fabrics and jewels (Byrne, 2012).

A telling example of Cervantes's indirect and subtle critique of contemporary leaders is found in a cogent letter that Don Quixote sent to Sancho after he assumed his role of Governor of the Island of Barataria. The letter provided perspicacious insights on the science and art of public administration for Sancho and satirical admonishments to the nonfictional leaders of the time from a safe distant and in a safe manner. As if speaking to the masses, Don Quixote penned to Sancho,

> Do not issue many decrees, and when you do, see to it that they are good ones and, above all, that they are observed and fulfilled, for decrees that are not observed are as none at all but, rather, convey the impression that the prince who had the wisdom and authority requisite for issuing them has not had the power to enforce them, and laws that merely hold a threat without being put into execution are like the log that was king of the frogs: at first he frightened them, but in time they came to despise him and mounted upon him.
>
> (Cervantes, 1604/1998, p. 1000)

The "history" of the *Man of La Mancha* is, like many fictional histories, replete with contradictions and varying perspectives found in society. Cervantes uses *Don Quixote* as a satire to cryptically speak truth to power and confront problematic features of society. Cervantes taught that judiciously challenging the status quo is a leadership act and that wise leaders institute change in the right measure to ensure that followers are neither too tightly controlled nor too easily ensnared by duplicative and vague rules and standards.

Wisdom

Don Quixote is a book about virtue. Don Quixote sets out on noble pursuits and models grit in his endurance through hardships. The mediating virtue of all other virtues is wisdom – discerning the right things to do (i.e., a transcendent wisdom often referred to by the Greeks as *sophia*) and doing them rightly (practical wisdom often referred to by the Greeks as *phronesis* and translated as prudence). *Don Quixote* is filled with proverbs in the context of the dramas within the story, making the proverbs come alive. Putnam (1604/1998) flagged 198 proverbs in the novel, an average of one proverb every 7.73 pages. While Don Quixote and Sancho did not consistently demonstrate skill at living well, they did rely on wisdom to discern which paths to pursue and how to successfully navigate the chosen adventures. Readers are repeatedly confronted with words of wisdom to reflect on how they should live life. Cervantes illustrated that the ability to cite and practice multiple proverbs provided a helpful foundation to eventually become skilled at living and leading, underscoring the power of the Don Quixote effect – people become what occupies their mind.

The prevalence of proverbs becomes comical at some points in the story, but none-the-less transformative, illustrated by Sancho's unanticipated success as the Governor of the Isle of Barataria. Sancho's curate could not "help believing that every member of the Panza family was born with a bagful of proverbs inside him; I never saw one that did not spill them at all hours and on every occasion" (Cervantes, 1604/1998, p. 994). Even Sancho reflected that he knew "more old sayings than would fill a book" (Cervantes, 1604/1998, p. 930). Cervantes illustrated how useful it is for leaders to have at their command "wise maxims drawn from long experience" (Cervantes, 1604/1998, p. 405) to inform their leadership conversations and practices so that they can govern judiciously. The command of so many maxims served Sancho well as the Governor of the Isle Barataria. His chief steward at the time noted,

> I am indeed astonished to hear a man wholly unlettered, as I believe your Grace to be, uttering so many wise maxims and observations, all of which is quite contrary to what was expected of your Grace's intelligence by those who sent us and by us who came here with you. Each day new things are seen in this world, jests are turned into earnest and the jesters are mocked.
>
> (Cervantes, 1604/1998, p. 978)

Cervantes frequent use of proverbs illustrated for his readers the value and nature of wisdom to live and lead well, making *Don Quixote* a book of lessons and instructions for the "adornment of the soul."[2] For example, Don Quixote provided the following advice to Sancho Panza just as he was about to assume his governorship.

> Eat sparingly during the day and have a light supper, for it is in the workshop of the stomach that the health of the entire body is forged. Be temperate in drinking, remembering that he who imbibes too much wine keeps neither secret nor promise. And take care, Sancho, not to roll our food from one cheek to the other or to eruct in front of anyone.
> (Cervantes, 1604/1998, p. 929)

Don Quixote continued,

> Observe moderation in the matter of sleep, for he who is not up with the sun does not make the most of the day. Bear in mind, Sancho, that diligence is the mother of good fortune, and sloth, its contrary, never yet achieved anything worthwhile.
> (Cervantes, 1604/1998, p. 930)

Cervantes demonstrates that wisdom is essential for leaders and followers to lead and follow well. Fullan (2001) wrote that "The more complex society gets, the more sophisticated leadership must become" (p. ix). A required, yet often elusive, component to people's *sophistication* is the attainment and use of wisdom as suggested by the etymology of the word (possession of *sophia* = Greek for wisdom). Stories of leaders' lack of discernment abound in the news. The frequent comments by subordinates of "what were they thinking?" and "why did they do that?" reveal that wisdom is often perceived to be lacking from those in formal leadership roles. Schwartz and Sharpe (2010) documented in their book *Practical Wisdom: The Right Way to Do the Right Thing* the decline in practical wisdom and its devastating consequences. The world needs people who judiciously discern and courageously implement innovative decisions at the right time and in the right way, people who pursue and practice wisdom.

The nature of governing

Sancho's dream of becoming governor of a small province is realized near the end of the story through an elaborate ruse by the Duke and Duchess. Sancho is given the governorship of the Isle Barataria. Cervantes noted that no one knew the exact provenance of the Isle's name since it was either named after the town or because the word *barato* means "low price" – reflecting the cost of the territory. Sancho, however, makes the most of the opportunity afforded him.

Sancho demonstrated his prowess as a governor, much to the surprise of those who knew him best, when sitting in judgment over disputes that his subjects brought before him. Don Sancho Panza won the respect of his subjects early in his tenure as governor. His success reveals that the role of office can accelerate the maturation of a leader and "make the man." Even the narrator noted that

> All those who were acquainted with Sancho Panza were astonished at hearing him use such elegant language and did not know to what to attribute it unless it was that offices carrying grave responsibilities sharpened the wits of some men while in the case of others the effect was merely stupefying.
>
> (Cervantes, 1604/1998, p. 977)

Whether it was his repertoire of proverbs, the opportunity for office, or a combination of both, Sancho demonstrated Solomon-like wisdom[3] during his short tenure as governor to the amazement of those who knew his appointment was a joke as well as those who were not in on the ruse.

Cervantes, through Don Quixote's advice to Sancho Panza and the recounting of Sancho's experiences as the Governor, provides powerful commentary on the need for wisdom and the nature of hardships associated with governing – truths all leaders can appreciate. Chapters 42–51 and 53 are filled with insights, examples, instructions, and challenges associated with governing wisely. The lucid letter from Don Quixote to Sancho dated a few days in to Sancho's governorship provided advice all leaders and managers would do well to heed.

> Remember, Sancho, that if you employ virtue as your means and pride yourself on virtuous deeds, you will have no cause to envy the means possessed by princes and noble lords; for blood is inherited, but virtue is acquired, and virtue by itself alone has a worth that blood does not have.
>
> (Cervantes, 1604/1998, p. 925)

Reminiscent of Machiavelli's *The Prince* and the wisdom of Aristotle, the letter goes on to offer additional counsel similar to what Don Quixote provided to Sancho prior to his assuming the governorship:

> In order to win the good will of the people that you govern, ... Be a father to virtue and a stepfather to vice. Be not always strict nor always lenient but observe a middle course between these two extremes, for therein lies wisdom.
>
> (Cervantes, 1604/1998, pp. 999–1000)

As a prudent governor, Sancho did not care much for the trappings of the office and took the burden of governing too seriously – so seriously that it became the tipping point for him to resign after only seven days. Sancho's success as a governor, albeit a short tenure, illustrated that the office can make the person,[4] requires virtue, and is wearisome.

Five leadership and management lessons from Melville's *Moby-Dick*

Leadership presence

The first sentence in *Moby-Dick*, "Call me Ishmael" – is a strong imperative, very much different in tenor than, "My name is Ishmael" or "Please call me Ishmael." The assertive imperative inspires confidence, sparks curiosity, and serves as a call to action. Implied in any imperative is some sense of authority, that the sender has the right or privilege to make an imposition on the receiver. In this instance, the assumption is that Ishmael is a truthful narrator with a compelling, if not urgent, message. The imperative generates a sense of obligation that cannot be ignored. The literary device of the imperative in *Moby-Dick* illustrated the mystique of leadership, and while leaders do not walk about telling people, "Call me Leader," they are people of the imperative mood in that their presence commands a response. Sense of presence conveys leadership, even more than a title, such that people do not need an official position to command.

Erving Goffman (1956), in *The Presentation of Self in Everyday Life,* used the metaphor of theatre to capture how "presence" conveys information that defines and subsequently enacts social situations and expectations. According to Goffman, people glean clues from the conduct and appearance of others, especially leaders, to navigate perceived social roles. Ishmael's introduction in the form of an imperative asserts his credibility as a narrator, at least initially, and sets the stage for what is about to unfold. In a very real sense, leaders are narrators like Ishmael and communicate in the imperative mood by their presence.

For Limardi, Morrison, and Morrison (2014), presence is associated with gravitas, confidence, and the ability to command a room. In their interviews with executives, they found four characteristics that defined executive presence – seriousness of purpose, ability to forge relationships on trust, strong personal connection, and focused awareness. According to Su and Wilkins (2013) in their book, *Own the Room: Discover Your Signature Voice to Master Your Leadership Presence,* leadership presence "is the ability to consistently and clearly articulate your value proposition while influencing and connecting with others" (p. 2). Baldoni (2010) in his book, *12 Steps to Power*

Presence: How to Assert Your Authority to Lead, defined leadership presence "as the presence of authority imbued with a reason to believe . . . it is a projection of the leader's authentic self" (p. 11). He went on to state that "all technical capabilities being equal, presence is what sets true leaders apart" (p. 2).

Lubar and Halpern (2004) in their book, *Leadership Presence* revealed that the mystique of presence can be learned and used their experience with the theatre and actors to ascertain what leads to a strong stage presence. They stated that "the skills that actors use to move, convince, inspire, or entertain have direct and powerful applications in the worlds of business, politics, education, and organizations in general" (p. 6). They elaborated how presence involves establishing authentic connections and being appropriately expressive, self-knowing, and in the moment. Dagley and Gasikin (2014) found ten characteristics of people who possess executive presence – status/reputation, physical appearance, projected confidence, communication ability, engagement skills, interpersonal integrity, values-in-action, intellect and expertise, outcome delivery ability, and coercive power. The authors noted that "the first five characteristics seemed to reflect the impressions formed during brief contacts . . . and the second five characteristics appeared to be related to evaluations formed during extended periods of contact" (p. 204).

Captain Ahab was an imposing captain whose weathered features and a whalebone leg conveyed that he was a man of experience and resolve. In Chapter 28, Ishmael described Ahab's presence "while he stood erect, looking straight out . . . with an infinity of firmest fortitude, unsurrenderable willfulness, and fixed and fearless dedication . . . in all the nameless, regal overbearing dignity of some mighty woe" (Melville, 1851/2007, p. 126). Unfortunately, Ahab's "presence," while captivating, belied his ulterior motives and hubris. We learn from Ahab that leadership presence with hubris has devastating consequences.

Hubris and white whales

All leaders have their equivalent of Ahab's white whale, a vision that enthuses them with passion and that focuses their efforts. Confidence and resolve are essential characteristics of leadership. The story of Ahab, however, provides a vivid lesson on what happens when ambition is motivated or informed by hubris.

Petit and Bollaert (2012), *Flying Too Close to the Sun? Hubris Among CEOs and How to Prevent It*, documented the all too common relationship between CEO hubris and corporate failures. Successful leaders dream and dare big and are drawn to go higher with each success. Petit and Bollaert described how the hubris syndrome is "an acquired condition" and is "triggered by accession to a position of power" (p. 266). According to the authors, to counter inflation of ego, leaders need to discipline themselves to remain grounded through self-awareness, balanced processing, moral action and virtue, and relational transparency, habits that eluded Ahab.

The distinctions among self-confidence, arrogance, and hubris are very fine (Owens, Wallace, & Waldman, 2015; Picone, Dagnino, & Mina, 2014). Self-confidence involves a realistic appraisal of one's abilities and provides one with a level of discernment and assurance to act as needed. Arrogance is thinking more highly of oneself and emboldens people to lead. At the same time arrogance creates blinders to make one ignorant of risks. Hubris is a reckless pride, acting as if one is god-like and therefore invulnerable (Strong, 2011).

The leadership literature is filled with treatises on the dark side of leadership and warnings against pride and hubris. Silverman, Johnson, McConnell, & Carr's (2012), *Arrogance: A Formula for Leadership Failure* empirically documented a negative correlation between performance and organizational citizenship. They cited research establishing that those who act superior usually have inferior performance and tend to have relatively lower cognitive abilities and self-esteem. Herbst (2014) in his book, *The Dark Side of Leadership* noted, "The subject of narcissism lies at the heart of leadership because a degree of narcissism is a prerequisite for climbing the corporate ladder" (p. 202). De Haan (2016) in his article, *The Leadership Shadow: How to Recognize and Avoid Derailment, Hubris and Overdrive,* described how people with power are vulnerable to a dark side of leadership. He astutely observed that

> leadership positions afford power in the form of the *managerial discretion* to act or hold sway one way or the other. Too much discretion or unchecked power allows our naturally selfish tendencies and self-confidence to grow and lead to the direction of abuse or leadership derailment.
>
> (p. 511)

De Haan (2016) goes on to state that

> failure to restrain the demons *within*, i.e. the leadership shadow, can result in a toxic organization and to very costly and bruising adjustments. Appreciating the benefits of certain attributes, whilst understanding when they tip into shadow side characteristics provides the key to actively managing them, reducing the risk to the organization as well as the risk of personal leadership derailment.
>
> (p. 511)

Ahab is the epitome of hubris and serves as a warning for all leaders to be vigilant. The root of Ahab's hubris was a denial of reality, the illusion that he was the sole captain of his destiny and those of his shipmates, unconstrained by the limits of nature. *Moby-Dick* illustrated that despite man's ability to explain and manipulate nature (look at all science had accomplished, even how to kill the leviathans such as whales) man is not in sole control, despite the lessons from the Enlightenment and advances in science and prominent evidence to the contrary (i.e., Ahab's whale-bone leg).

The counter to hubris is an authentic humility. Standish (2007) provided a thought-provoking article titled, *Whatever Happened to Humility: Rediscovering a Misunderstood Leadership Strength*. Standish used the example of Gandhi to illustrate that one can be both humble and a leader. Argandona (2015) explained how humility is not necessarily prized in the business world and lost its luster due to an overemphasis on self-reliance. Waldman and Bowen (2016) highlighted the paradox of a strong sense of self (self-concept and self-efficacy) and humility (admitting incompleteness and interdependence). Collins (2001) found that among companies that went from good to great, there were a group of executive leaders who demonstrated a "paradoxical blend of personal humility and professional will," what he identified as Level 5 Leaders (p. 22). These were people who sincerely focused on the success of the organization in contrast to the pursuit of fame and fortune. Collins astutely noted how the business world fails to promote, if even notice, emerging leaders who lack hubris:

> The great irony is the animus and personal ambition that often drive people to positions of power stand at odds with the humility required for Level 5 leadership. When you combine that irony with the fact that boards of directors frequently operate under the false belief that they need to hire a larger-than-life, egocentric leader to make the organization great, you can quickly see why Level 5 leaders rarely appear at the top of our institutions.
>
> (pp. 36–37)

Humility and strength can and should go together. Theodore Roosevelt delivered his "National Duties – Big Stick" speech at the Minnesota State Fair on September 2, 1901.[5] The following portion of the speech captures the synergistic effect of combining presence (carry a big stick) with humility (speak softly), in a motto that would define Roosevelt's presidency.

> The good many of you are probably acquainted with the old proverb, "Speak softly and carry a big stick – you will go far." If a man continually blusters, if he lacks civility, a big stick will not save him

from trouble, and either will speaking softly avail, if back of softness there does not lie strength, power. In private life there are few being more obnoxious than the man who is always loudly boasting, and if the boaster is not prepared to back up his powers, his position becomes absolute contemptible. So it is with the nation. It is both foolish and undignified to indulge in undue self-glorification, and above all, in loose-tongued denunciation of other people.

(Welter, 2014)

Just as Ahab demonstrated the peril of hubris associated with presence, Theodore Roosevelt demonstrated the wisdom of presence with humility.

Organizational leader-follower complicity

Life on a whaling ship as described in *Moby-Dick* captured the principles of classical organizational and institutional theories before those developed by social scientists like Weber, Taylor, Follett, Mayo, and Selznick. Melville described in detail the hierarchical structure and division of labor necessary to efficiently hunt and harvest whales. He highlighted how group norms formed and shaped roles and expectations beyond what the formal structure dictated. The *Pequod* was a residential factory. It brought to the forefront the extreme conditions of factory life beginning to populate the American landscape. On the *Pequod* the crew willingly gives up three years away from home to serve at the pleasure of others in unpleasant, harsh, menial, and at times dangerous work.

Moby-Dick also illustrated the toxic triangle of destructive leaders, susceptible followers, and conducive environments (Padilla, Hogan, & Kaiser, 2007). Leaders do not operate in a vacuum. Leaders emerge because followers grant them authority and power to act on their behalf. Certain environments and types of followers enable dysfunctional leaders, promote selective moral disengagement (Bandura, 2002), and coopt organizational goals for personal agendas (Thoroughgood, Padilla, Hunter, & Tatee, 2012).

Kets de Vries (2001) described the symbiotic relationship between leaders and followers as a form of collusion. Leaders and followers enable each other to shape their respective organizational dramas. The crew could have decided to hold Ahab in check, but rather they became complicit.[6] Ahab acknowledged this when he bribed the crew to pursue Moby Dick at all costs by appealing to their venal tendencies.

Whosoever of ye raises me a white-headed whale with a wrinkled brow and a crooked jaw; whosoever of ye raises me that white-headed whale, with three holes punctured in his starboard fluke—look ye, whosoever of ye raises me that same white whale, he shall have this gold ounce, my boys!

(Melville, 1851/2007, p. 159)

Bratton, Grint, and Nelson (2004) described how followers provide "destructive consent" when they acquiesce to problematic behavior. Thoroughgood et al. (2012) documented follower susceptibility and compliance tendencies and concluded that "No matter how clever or devious, leaders alone cannot achieve toxic results" (p. 901). Destructive leaders are incapable of carrying out their toxic agendas without the assistance of susceptible followers and conducive environments.

Kellerman (2008) emphasized in her book, *Followership: How Followers are Creating Change and Changing Leaders*, why and how subordinates' behavior shapes their leaders' behavior. Since followers have relative power, Kellerman asked, "Why do we go along with bad leaders instead of doing them in? Why not just wrest from them the capacity to exert power, wield authority, and exercise influence, and replace them with leaders who are better?" (p. 60). In addition to the typical individual and group reasons that followers go along with their leaders, Kellerman provided the following justifications why people defer to bad leaders:

- The sequential nature of following, whereby small acts of going along lead gradually to a significant commitment.
- The social nature of following, whereby the behavior of the other followers encourages people to do what they would not do otherwise.
- The "agentic" nature of following, whereby followers blame others, usually superiors, for acts they committed.
- The ideological nature of following, whereby people are persuaded the end justifies the means (pp. 60–61).

Unless followers exercise options for timely exits or have courage to stage a mutiny, they are by default part of the leadership team and are part responsible for their leaders' behavior. While some followers may be innocent, or pseudo-innocent,[7] of direct complicity, all followers indirectly share in their leaders' folly. Melville highlighted by the absence of examples in the novel that followers need to be shrewd and innocent as doves[8] to bring about change in asymmetric power relationships.

Given that followers at any time can undermine their leaders' credibility and authority, leaders must attend to, or at minimum appease, the values and expectations imposed upon them or risk dethronement, a coup, or in Ahab's case – a mutiny. Just as political leaders follow the polls to tailor their campaigns to win elections, all leaders must continually fine-tune their agenda to address the needs, expectations, and behaviors of their followers. At the same time, leaders serving under hubristic superiors must discern when and how to manage their boss so as to circumvent a destruction of the organization.

Ultimacy

Moby-Dick questioned and challenged taken-for-granted assumptions about people's ultimate purpose and place in the universe. Melville used *Moby-Dick* to explore religious and metaphysical themes related to mortality, fate, and humans' relationship to God, nature, and each other. The tone is set right from the start in Chapter 1 with the title, *Loomings*. Ishmael also takes time to describe the universal mystical appeal of water to provide a sense of tranquility and transcendence as a cure from the hardships of life on the land.

Certain Christian sensibilities are found lacking when they are juxtaposed with the "savage" Queequeg's gracious thoughts and actions. Melville used Father Mapple's sermon to unpack the theology and implications from the story of Jonah. Readers are challenged to identify and confront falsehoods and live accordingly in obedience to the Almighty. The relationship between the Christian Ishmael and the "heathen" Queequeg demonstrated that "ignorance is the parent of fear" (Melville, 1851/2007, p. 38). Ignorance fuels prejudice, and true love is the remedy as stated by Melville, "yet see how elastic our prejudices grow when once love comes to bend them" (p. 66). Ishmael and Queequeg met a strange man by the name of Elijah who warned them of their fate on the *Pequod* and asked if they considered to whom and what they sold their souls.

Melville highlighted the happenstances and vicissitudes of life in the plot among the different characters, documenting how the crew was at the mercy of Ahab, and how Ahab was at the mercy of nature. Even the Biblical names that Melville assigned his characters provided ominous connotations.

- Ishmael, the son of Abraham and Hagar and half-brother to Isaac. Isaac became God's appointed heir to the Abrahamic covenant while Ishmael was sent into exile with God's protection (Genesis 16 and 21).
- Ahab, a king of Israel who turned from God to worship Baal and who "did evil in the sight of the Lord more than all who were before him" (I Kings 16:30).
- Elijah, an Old Testament prophet who spoke against King Ahab and who asked "how long will you [the people of Israel] hesitate between two opinions" (I Kings 18:21) in the classic contest between Baal and Yahweh.

Both *Moby-Dick* and Melville's life concluded with cruel endings and irony. Ishmael was the only crewmember to survive on a makeshift life raft from an unused coffin. Melville, an enlightened author with a short tenure of relative notoriety, worked 20 unadventurous years on the docks in relative obscurity as an unhappy recluse.

A more profound lesson from *Moby-Dick* is the value of engaging in the existential questions of life in the workplace. Organizations that fail to resolve transcendent questions and concerns risk the same fate as the *Pequod*. The *Pequod*, like all organizational settings, became a stressful work environment that required a unique level of immersion. Briskin (1998) noted that "the more immersed we become in the workplace, the less of ourselves is available to the full continuum of living" (p. 184) both to the demise of the individual and organization (i.e., the *Pequod* is eventually destroyed). While the *Pequod* was a ship, it was also a factory and a metaphor for the contemporary organizations of the 19th century. Melville portrayed the crew wrestling with their corporate and personal identities and brought to the forefront the alienation that comes from separating the two. While most organizations do not require total abandonment of one's personal life like the *Pequod*, organizational settings can't but at times have a depersonalizing effect, especially when the stakes are high.

Briskin (1998) in his award-winning book, *Stirring of Soul in the Workplace* based upon his 20 years as an organizational consultant reported that far too many work environments feel dehumanizing as employees have divided loyalties and identities. According to Briskin, "no one can mature in a culture or organization without internalizing aspects of it. We are by nature dependent on family, community, social institutions, and our workplaces for our survival and to a large extent our sense of identity" (p. 65). This requires people to continually evaluate who they are and are becoming as they manage their multiple selves. Since work and career occupy the major percentage of a working adult's time, unless one is careful, organizations become keepers of individual souls (p. 66).

Briskin (1998) defined the soul as the "multiplicity of selves within each us; their interactions and struggles are the threads that weave the self together" (p. 5). Organizations risk becoming soulless when they marginalize human considerations. Briskin noted that organizations have a dilemma in honoring the multidimensionality of employees "without simply molding people to group aims" and people have the dilemma to "retain more of ourselves" without losing themselves to the organization (p. 66).

Education – my Yale and Harvard

Herman Melville was well read and self-educated, as evidenced by his detailed scientific, literary, theological, and philosophical references in *Moby-Dick*. The books and lessons from his prominent grandparents on both sides provided Melville early exposure and an appreciation for learning necessary to hold an upper standing in society consistent with his heritage. A formal education in his early years provided a foundation and requisite understanding of the metaphysics and rhetoric that would inform his future learning and writings. A reversal of fortunes that his family experienced when he was a child and the loss of his father provided Melville a crash course on the crueler side of fate that dominated *Moby-Dick*.

Yet it was his time at sea that Melville's education would be complete, reflected in the allusion to himself in words of Ishmael, "for a whale-ship was my Yale College and my Harvard" (Melville, 1851/2007, p. 114). Parker (1996) observed that "Melville had ample time for absorbing literary treatments" being exposed to variety of books found among the various ships' libraries, where Melville did more reading than actual sailing or whaling (p. 234). The three and half years at life at sea and on exotic islands, interaction with a variety of foreigners, and access to books and the discretionary time to read them provided Melville a unique and thorough education (Parker, 1996). Bryant and Springer (2007) gave evidence of Melville being well read:

> We do know that Melville carried with him a trunk-load of books [Melville traveled to and from London in 1850], including works by dramatists (Jonson, Davenant, Marlowe, Beaumont and Fletcher, and Shakespeare), romantics (Rousseau, Goethe, De Quincy, Lamb), and gothicists (Horace Walpole and Mary Shelley). Also in the trunk were Boswell's *Life of Johnson*, Sir Thomas Bowen's *Vulgar Errors*, various guidebooks, Lavater's book on phrenology and more. References to nearly all of these works are scattered throughout *Moby-Dick*, and is safe to say that Melville's reading in them, either at sea or back home, helped him shape his whale narrative, including its plot.
>
> (p. ix)

It was for this reason that Melville would and could claim through Ishmael that he had an alternate "Yale and Harvard." Unfortunately, the great questions Melville raised in *Moby-Dick* as a self-taught man in theology, philosophy, and science failed to provide him solace and peace in the latter part of his life to celebrate the kinder side of fate and God's benevolence.

Melville demonstrated that all of life is an apprenticeship for the next stage, and how well one does at the current stage determines subsequent doors of opportunity and future apprenticeships. Melville's self-taught education also reinforced the theme of this book, reading deeply and broadly across fields of interests serves one well.

Two leadership and management lessons from *Pride and Prejudice*

One could easily wonder how a satirical romance novel such as *Pride and Prejudice* should be included in a book bridging literature with management and leadership. As with all good works of literature, it addresses several universal themes and provides an endearing commentary for leaders and managers to gain some emotional and social intelligence that will serve them well in the workplace. Specifically, Austen demonstrated that virtuous people make for good protagonists and are better equipped to overcome pride and vanity when it surfaces.

Improved perspectives, language, and behaviors

The elevated opinions and intelligent prose of the lead characters are in part attributed to their reading habits, not solely from their station in life. For the most part, the hero and heroine of the story demonstrate a comportment that sets them apart from the other characters in the book. Miss Elizabeth Bennet and Mr. Fitzwilliam Darcy were not bothered by the trivialities of life as many of the other characters who were not as well read. For example, early in the story a conversation ensued on what makes an accomplished woman. Mr. Darcy noted that above all of the qualities listed in the conversation, "and to all this she must add something more substantial, in the improvement of her mind by extensive reading" (Austen, 1813/2003, p. 40). Jane Austen used this conversation to underscore her conviction that being well read is an important component to being an accomplished individual, a conviction that was even more dominant in her novel, *Mansfield Park* where she also penned that "fondness for reading, properly directed, must be an education in itself" (Austen, 1814/1970, p. 19).[9]

Elizabeth proved herself "quite equal" (Austen, 1813/2003, p. 162) to her new circle of acquaintances in the upper class of society, in part attributed to her improved mind. Elizabeth was able to verbally spar with Mr. Darcy and others with a vocabulary and wit not typically found by those in her station. Elizabeth's backhanded rebukes in her exchanges with Lady Catherine DeBourgh, the pretentious antagonist in the story, demonstrated that she would neither conform to limited expectations of her class nor assume subservient roles like several other characters in the book. This becomes most evident when Lady Catherine arrives unexpectedly at the Bennet house to demand that Elizabeth refuse a pending, albeit, rumored, marriage proposal from her nephew, Mr. Darcy.

In their final encounter in the book, the incredulous Lady Catherine let Elizabeth know that she would not be trifled with. Throughout the conversations, Lady Catherine took umbrage at Elizabeth's insolence. Lady Catherine attempted, to no avail, to use her nobility to put Elizabeth in her place with such statements as, "Miss Bennet, do you know who I am? I have not been accustomed to such language as this" (Austen, 1813/2003, p. 343) and "Obstinate, headstrong girl! I am ashamed of you! Is this your gratitude for my attentions to you last spring? Is nothing due to me on this score?" (Austen, 1813/2003, p. 344). Elizabeth brought an end to the conversation by not yielding to Lady Catherine's demand, declaring that "I am only resolve to act in that manner, which will, in my opinion, constitute my happiness, without reference to you, or to any person so wholly unconnected to me" (Austen, 1813/2003, p. 346).

Elizabeth's composure, sophistication with words, and ability to turn Lady Catherine's words against her, proved that Elizabeth was not one to trifle with either. Elizabeth became an example of how to respectfully speak truth to power and models the wisdom of King Solomon – "If the ruler's temper rises against you, do not abandon your position, because composure allays great offenses" (Ecclesiastes 10:4 New American Standard Version).

Another example of a most composed exchange of thoughts transpired between Elizabeth and Mr. Darcy on the occasion of his unsolicited marriage proposal to her. Elizabeth turned down Mr. Darcy's first marriage proposal with a gracious rebuke and collected manner when lesser minds would have accepted a poorly worded proposal just to secure a better station in life, regardless of love. After receiving an unwelcome reply to his proposal, Mr. Darcy inquired "in a voice of forced calmness" why there was "little endeavor at civility," even though more incivility seemed easily warranted given Elizabeth's misperception of injustices perpetrated by Mr. Darcy toward her sister and a family friend. Elizabeth proceeded to outline why she had "every reason in the world to think ill" of Mr. Darcy (Austen, 1813/2003, p. 189). The subsequent dialog, although based upon lies and misinformation, was candid, yet composed without the vitriolic words and tenor one would expect from those less civil and not bounded by any sense of propriety. Mr. Darcy said goodnight with so much unsaid only because his genteel code of conduct required him to exercise restraint, lest he said something in the heat of the moment that he would later regret – not wanting to wound Elizabeth with the truth in such a vulnerable moment.

The next day Mr. Darcy provided Elizabeth a lengthy letter with well-chosen words and poetic flow that addressed the two offenses that Elizabeth had laid against him the previous day. Mr. Darcy went into great detail and with a gentle tenor to reframe the facts behind Elizabeth's judgments. Mr. Darcy made it clear that he was not writing to win her hand in marriage, but to provide a full telling of the stories to vindicate his honor and free Elizabeth of her ignorance. The letter becomes a model of how to fluently speak the truth with eloquence, patience and sensitivity, even in the heat of tragic misunderstandings and mischaracterizations. The letter was a turning point in the story and revealed that well-chosen words said at the right time in the right tenor ultimately triumphs.

Elizabeth and Mr. Darcy's composure, discretion, and principled thoughts yielded uncompromising civility that endeared them so many people. Austen demonstrated that the protagonists' emotional and social intelligence were in part developed by their reading habits. Leaders, managers, and employees at all levels in a work environment should cultivate a sophisticated understanding of people and culture through books so as to be equally skilled at engaging others.

It is worthwhile to note that Jane Austen's characters were capable of sophisticated thoughts and noble actions in part because Jane was an avid reader herself. She was fortunate to have access to her father's library and that of a family friend. Dow and Halsey (2010) documented that Jane Austen read extensively while growing up and even regretted not reading more in her youth. They stated that

> The cultural resonance of books allows Austen to use them as a sort of convenient shorthand to help her readers swiftly understand her characters. Cultural commentators of Austen's period frequently suggested that "we are what we read." In Austen's novels, it might be truer to say that how we use what we read defines us.

Jane Austen, Mr. Darcy, and Elizabeth Bennet are additional evidence that people become what they read and that great literature, when rightly availed, is a masterful tutor and mentor to become skilled at living (Sample, 2001). Familiarity with great literature provided the three with eloquence and enlightened perspectives to successfully navigate themselves, others, and circumstances. Similarly, as documented in Chapter 4, it equally schooled certain business and political leaders to be especially astute and skilled in their sensemaking leadership practices.

The role of literature as a source for acquiring elevated perspectives is akin to what Heifetz and Linsky (2002) described as taking a balcony view when leading. In their insightful book, *Leadership on the Line: Staying Alive through the Dangers of Leading*, they noted that "few practical ideas are more obvious or more critical than the need to get perspective in the midst of action" (p. 51). They used the metaphor of "getting off the dance floor and going to the balcony" to express how leaders need to regularly distance themselves from the fray to engage in important sensemaking observations and reflections.

This perspective-taking exercise is especially important given that leadership is an extremely taxing endeavor that far too easily robs leaders of the joys and enthusiasms associated with leading. Heifetz and Linsky revealed why leadership is dangerous and how well-intended people often self-destruct. They provided practical suggestions for leaders to effectively lead complex organizations (i.e., make leading a bit more manageable) and remain anchored. A big takeaway from Heifetz and Linsky is that leaders must be diligent to maintain elevated perspectives if they are to thrive in their leadership endeavors. As demonstrated above and in Chapter 4, reading great literature equips leaders with a grand view of both the balcony and dance floor so as to lead with eloquence and more enlightened and elevated perspectives, without which, renders them less effective and more vulnerable to derailment.

Pride and vanity

Upon their first meeting, Elizabeth Bennet and her family found Mr. Darcy "to be only just tolerable" (Austen, 1813/2003, p. 20). The rumor about the newcomer to the Bennet community was that Mr. Darcy was "ate up with pride" (Austen, 1813/2003, p. 20). The early gossip around the taciturn Mr. Darcy generated explicit and contradictory insights on the nature of pride. On the one hand, while Elizabeth found pride to be contemptible, Miss Lucas, believed Mr. Darcy had "a right to be proud" (Austen, 1813/2003, p. 21) given all that was in his favor. Elizabeth's sister Mary observed that

> Pride, . . . is a very common failing, I believe. By all that I have ever read, I am convinced that is very common indeed, that human nature is particularly prone to it, . . . Vanity and pride are different things, though the words are used synonymously. A person may be proud without being vain. Pride relates more to our opinion of ourselves; vanity to what we would have others think of us.
>
> (Austen, 1813/2003, p. 21)

Mary's insights established two themes in *Pride and Prejudice* that abound in organizational settings, especially competitive work and marketing environments; first being pleased with one's abilities and accomplishments without thinking more highly about oneself, and second being reputable without guile and/or showing off. Regarding the latter theme, people and businesses manage impressions to tilt social interactions in a favorable direction. Goffman (1956) introduced the concept of impression management in his seminal book, *The Presentation of Self in Everyday Life*. Goffman used the metaphor of theater to capture how people are at one level performers who manage impressions to create desired social realities. There is a profound difference between building a reputation and chasing a reputation. When what others think defines people and their subsequent actions, then that fine line between sincere and contrived performances has been crossed, making performers in social settings prone to mislead for favorable, albeit false, opinions.

Vain deference to public opinion is problematic and something to be avoided when valued principles are at stake. The final interaction between Lady Catherine and Elizabeth provided insight to the nature of vanity. As previously referenced, Lady Catherine was agitated with Elizabeth's obstinate and headstrong refusal to acknowledge her intent to decline or accept a pending second marriage proposal from her nephew. Elizabeth asked Lady Catherine why she should not accept Mr. Darcy. Lady Catherine replied,

> Because honour, decorum, prudence, nay interest, forbid it. Yes, Miss Bennet, interest; for do not expect to be noticed by his family or friends if you willfully act against the inclinations of all. You will be censured, slighted, and despised, by everyone connected with him. Your alliance will be a disgrace; your name will never be mentioned by any of us.
>
> (Austen, 1813/2003, p. 344)

Unfazed by the strong sentiment, Elizabeth replied, "These are heavy misfortunes, but the wife of Mr. Darcy must have such extraordinary sources of happiness necessarily attached to her situation, that she could, upon the whole, have no cause to repine" (Austen, 1813/2003, p. 344).

Pride is also problematic when peoples' opinions of themselves make them haughty. Elizabeth's epiphany upon full knowledge of the facts that led to her false characterization of Mr. Darcy revealed the self-deception and destruction that comes with pride. Upon reflection of the letter and reevaluation of the facts, Elizabeth realized that she acted despicably.

> I who prided myself on my discernment! I, who have valued myself on my abilities! who have often disdained the generous candour of my sister, and gratified my vanity in useless or blamable distrust. How humiliating is this discovery! Yet, how just a humiliation! Had I been in love, I could not have been more wretchedly blind. But vanity, not love, has been my folly. Pleased with the preference of one, and offended by the neglect of the other, on the very beginning of our acquaintance, I have courted prepossession [prejudice] and ignorance, and driven reason away where either were concerned. Till this moment, I never knew myself.
>
> (Austen, 1813/2003, pp. 204–205)

Mr. Darcy also had an epiphany about his pride which he found repre-
hensible. The now newly betrothed are on a walk reflecting on their circumstances and personal growth that led to their union after a false start.
Mr. Darcy observed,

> What did you say of me that I did not deserve? For though your accusa-
> tions were ill-founded, formed on mistaken premises, my behaviour to
> you at the time had merited the severest reproof. It was unpardonable.
> I cannot think of it without abhorrence.
>
> (Austen, 1813/2003, p. 355)

After Elizabeth attempts to reassure him, Mr. Darcy continued,

> I cannot be so easily reconciled to myself. The recollection of what
> I then said, of my conduct, my manners, my expressions during the
> whole of it, is now, and has been many months, inexpressibly painful
> to me. Your reproof, so well applied, I shall never forget: 'Had you
> behaved in a more gentlemanlike manner'.
>
> (Austen, 1813/2003, p. 355)

> . . . . I have been a selfish being all my life, in practice, though not in
> principle. As a child I was taught what was *right*, but I was not taught to
> correct my temper. I was given good principles, but left to follow them
> in pride and conceit.
>
> (Austen, 1813/2003, p. 357)

Mr. Darcy's confession revealed that his principled pride made him
haughty. The good news is that pride and prejudice do not have to be permanent. Elizabeth and Mr. Darcy demonstrated that personal growth is
possible. Mr. Darcy and Elizabeth became social mirrors to each other's
ignorance. Mr. Darcy reflected such in his confession to Elizabeth,

> Such I was, from eight to eight-and-twenty; and such I might still have
> been but for you, dearest, loveliest Elizabeth! What do I not owe you!
> You taught me a lesson, hard indeed at first, but most advantageous.
> By you, I was properly humbled. I came to you without a doubt of my
> reception. You showed me how insufficient were all my pretensions to
> please a woman worthy of being pleased.
>
> (Austen, 1813/2003, p. 357)

The leadership and management literature is filled with research on
pride and humility. As cited above with Ahab's hubris, Collins (2001)

research in *From Good to Great*, showed that leaders of great organizations demonstrate a profound sense of humility. Schellenbarger's (2018) Wall Street Journal Article, *The Best Bosses are Humble Bosses*, described how humility is one of the most important traits for leaders, but ironically has been overshadowed by more self-promoting colleagues. Schellenbarger noted that,

> Humility is a core quality of leaders who inspire close teamwork, rapid learning and high performance in their teams, according to several studies in the past three years. Humble people tend to be aware of their own weaknesses, eager to improve themselves, appreciative of others' strengths and focused on goals beyond their own self-interest.

Possessing a special sense of fondness and appreciation toward one's self, family, work, and accomplishments is a form of honoring what is good. Such a position of honor though requires performers (to use Goffman's model) to guard against haughtiness and vanity.

It is worth noting that *Pride and Prejudice* highlighted a different manifestation of pride than what was emphasized in *Moby-Dick*. Ahab's pride was his hubris, a blind arrogance that led to a sense of invincibility. Mr. Darcy and Elizabeth's pride was their haughtiness, a discrete sense of superiority that led to prejudging others. Hubris and haughtiness are equally problematic, and if unchecked, both lead to destruction. The former is at times masked as arrogant ambition and the latter by principled convictions. Humility is the golden mean between hubris and timidity and between haughtiness and inferiority.

Summary and conclusion

Miguel de Cervantes, Herman Melville, and Jane Austen provided timeless leadership and followership lessons in their respective epic novels: *Don Quixote, Moby-Dick*, and *Pride and Prejudice*. Respectively, the three novels teach that emerging and established leaders would do well to tenaciously seek noble ambitions without tilting at windmills, pursue goals without hubris and forfeiting other organizational considerations, and conduct themselves in principled and elevated manners free from haughty and vain pretense. More generally, they challenge common and negative cultural assumptions and practices that would otherwise be left unquestioned. They illustrate the importance of informal and formal education in refining character. Above all, they provide insights to cultivate social and emotional intelligence through their detailed plots and the lives of the various characters in the context of their times and places.

While each novel provides explicit insights to leadership and management, individually and collectively they demonstrate the power of the narrative. Knowledge of novels equips readers with a language and vocabulary that can resonate and even inspire others, in contrast to those only educated on Dr. Seuss level vocabulary and style of rhetoric. Books, especially those that have stood the test of time, socialize leaders to the craft of fine storytelling and equip them to better understand the motivations of the protagonists, antagonists, and supporting characters in their organization. More importantly, novels such as *Don Quixote, Moby-Dick,* and *Pride and Prejudice* provide a lifetime of insights on the emotional, social, and transcendent considerations and plights that people bring to their work equipping readers with empathy to better engage the collective and create more humane and meaningful work environments.

Notes

1 Irish playwright, critic, polemicist and political activist during the 1800s. *Maxims for Revolutionists* is the appendix to Shaw's *Man and Superman: A Comedy and a Philosophy.*

2 Don Quixote stated to Sancho Panza, "What I have said to you thus far has been in the nature of instruction for the adornment of your soul" in reference to the series of advice related to being a good governor (Cervantes, 1604/1998, p. 927).

3 Solomon served as King of Israel from 971 to 931 BC. Upon his succession to the throne Solomon asked God for wisdom to rule the people effectively. His wisdom became so well known that foreign dignitaries traveled from afar to hear his wisdom (cf. I Kings 3–4).

4 This provides hope that even foolish individual like Sancho can be transformed to serve wisely when elected or appointed to an office, assuming that the individual, like Sancho, has a servant heart and a wealth of wise maxims to inform his or her thinking and practices.

5 Theodore Roosevelt would become President of the United States 12 days after the speech that would define his presidency. President William McKinley was at the Pan-American Exposition in Buffalo, New York when he was shot twice by a sole assassin and would die on September 14.

6 If the crew had successfully harvested Moby-Dick, the world would have judged Ahab and the crew as heroes. Society tends to evaluate motives based upon outcomes. The difference between a hero and fool is their respective success rates.

7 Rollo May (1972) in his book, *Power and Innocence,* contrasted true innocence with pseudo-innocence – an unwarranted naiveté that excuses one from claiming or exercising power to make a restorative difference in the collective. It is interesting to note that May uses Melville's story, *Billy Budd,* to illustrate that child-like innocence, while endearing, is a tragic flaw in the adult world.

8 When Jesus sent his disciples out to minister he told them to be prudent and pure in their interactions with those they met (i.e., be as shrewd as serpents and as innocent as doves). Matthew 10:16.

9 Kelly (1982) noted that "*Mansfield Park* is a novel of education, then, one might say of the romance of education" (p. 31). She goes on to state "*Mansfield Park* is about reading, then, about the nature of eloquence, silent and vocal, about the moral and ethical content of eloquence, about the institutional context of eloquence, and about its social effects. *Mansfield Park* is about reading as an act of the profoundest significance for his and her society" (p. 49). Kelly, G. (1982). Reading Aloud in *Mansfield Park*. *Nineteenth-century fiction, 37* (2), 29–49.

References

Argandona, A. (2015). Humility in management. *Journal of Business Ethics, 132*, 63–71.

Ariely, D. (2013). The honest truth about dishonesty: How we lie to everyone – Especially ourselves. New York, NY: HarperCollins Publishers.

Austen, J. (1813/2003). *Pride and prejudice.* New York, NY: Barnes & Noble Books (Original work published 1813).

Austen, J. (1814/1970). *Mansfield park.* New York, NY: Oxford University Press.

Baldoni, J. (2010). *12 Steps to power presence: How to assert your authority to lead.* Nashville, TN: AMACOM.

Bandura, A. (2002). Selective moral disengagement in the exercise of moral agency. *Journal of Moral Education, 31*(2), 101–119.

Bratton, J., Grint, K., & Nelson, D. (2004). *Organizational leadership.* Mason, OH: South Western/Thomson.

Briskin, A. (1998) *Stirring of soul in the workplace.* San Francisco, CA: Berrett-Koehler Publishers, Inc.

Bryant, J., & Springer, H. (2007) Introduction. In H. Melville (Ed.), *Moby Dick, A longman critical edition* (pp. vii–xxvi). London, England: Pearson Longman.

Byrne, S. (2012). *Law and history in Cervantes: Don Quixote.* Toronto, ON: University of Toronto Press.

Cervantes, S. M. (1604/1998). *Don Quixote* (S. Putnam, Trans.). New York, NY: Modern Library (Originally published 1604).

Chung-Ming, L., & Woodman, R. (1995). Understanding organizational change: A schematic perspective. *The Academy of Management Journal, 38*(2), 537–554.

Collins, J. (2001). *Good to great: Why some companies make the leap . . . and others don't.* New York, NY: HarperBusiness.

Dagley, G. R., & Gaskin, C. J. (2014). Understanding executive presence: Perspectives of business professionals. *Consulting Psychology Journal: Practice & Research, 66*(3), 197–211.

de Haan, E. (2016). The leadership shadow: How to recognize and avoid derailment, hubris and overdrive. *Leadership, 12*(4), 504–512.

Dow, G., & Halsey, K. (2010). Jane Austen's reading: The chawton years. *The Jane Austen Society of North America Persuasion Online Journal, 30*(2). Retrieved from http://www.jasna.org/persuasions/on-line/vol30no2/dow-halsey.html

Duckworth, A. (2016). *Grit: The power of passion and perseverance.* New York, NY: Scribner.

Fullan, M. (2001). *Leading in a culture of change.* San Francisco, CA: Jossey-Bass.

Goffman, E. (1956). *The presentation of self in everyday life.* New York, NY: DoubleDay.

Heifetz, R., & Linsky, M. (2002). *Leadership on the line: Staying alive through the dangers of leading.* Boston, MA: Harvard Business School Press.

Herbst, T. (2014). *The dark side of leadership.* Bloomington, IN: AuthorHouse.

Kellerman, B. (2008). *Followership: How followers are creating change and changing leaders.* Boston, MA: Harvard Business Press. ISBN: 978-1-4221-0368-5

Kets de Vries, M. F. R. (2001). *Struggling with the demon: Perspectives on individual and organizational irrationality.* Madison, CT: Psychosocial Press.

Kotter, J. P. (1990). What leaders really do? *Harvard Business Review, 68*(3), 103–111.

Kouzes, J., & Posner, B. (2012). *The leadership challenge: How to make extraordinary things happen in organizations* (5th ed.). San Francisco, CA: Jossey-Bass.

Limardi, D., Morrison, D., & Morrison. D. (2014, June). Executive presence: Do you have the leadership "wow" factor? *Public Management.* Retrieved from https://icma.org/documents/pm-magazine-june-2014

Lubar, K. & Halpern, B. (2004). *Leadership presence.* New York, NY: Avery.

Melville, H. (2007). *Moby Dick, A longman critical edition* (J. Bryant & H. Springer, Trans.). London, England: Pearson Longman (Original work published in 1851).

Owens, B. P., Wallace, A. S., & Waldman, D. A. (2015). Leader narcissism and follower outcomes: The counterbalancing effect of leader humility. *Journal of Applied Psychology, 100*(4), 1203–1213.

Padilla, A., Hogan, R., & Kaiser, R. B. (2007). The toxic triangle: Destructive leaders, susceptible followers, and conducive environments. *The Leadership Quarterly, 18*(3), 176–194.

Parker, H. (1996). *Herman Melville: A biography volume I, 1819–1851.* Baltimore, MD: The John Hopkins University Press.

Petit, V., & Bollaert, H. (2012). Flying too close to the sun? Hubris among CEOs and how to prevent it. *Journal of Business Ethics, 108*(3), 265–283. Retrieved from http://www.jstor.org/stable/41476294

Picone, P. M., Dagnino, G. B., & Mina, A. (2014). The origin of failure: A multidimensional appraisal of the hubris hypothesis and proposed research agenda. *The Academy of Management Perspectives, 28*(4), 447–468. http://dx.doi.org/10.5465/amp.2012.0177

Putnam, S. (2008). Introduction. In S. M. (Ed.), *Don Quixote* (1604/1998) (pp. xxiii–xxxiii). New York, NY: Modern Library (Originally published 1604).

Ryan, J. (2009, July 29). Leadership success always starts with vision. *Forbes.* Retrieved from https://www.forbes.com/2009/07/29/personal-success-vision-leadership-managing-ccl.html#3c75cfbc6634

Sample, S. (2001). *The contrarian's guide to leadership.* San Francisco, CA: Jossey-Bass.

Schellenbarger, S. (2018, October 9). The best bosses are humble bosses. *Wall Street Journal.* Retrieved from https://www.wsj.com/articles/the-best-bosses-are-humble-bosses-1539092123

Schwartz, B., & Sharpe, K. (2010). *Practical wisdom: The right way to do the right thing.* New York, NY: Penguin Group.

Shapiro, J., & Rucker, L. (2004). The Don Quixote effect: Why going to the movies can help develop empathy and altruism in medical students and residents. *Families, Systems & Health: The Journal of Collaborative Family Healthcare, 22*(4), 445–452.

Shaw, G. B. (1903). *Man and superman: A comedy and a philosophy.* Cambridge, MA: The University Press.

Shoup, J. R. (2005). *A collective biography of twelve world-class leaders: A study on developing exemplary leaders.* Lanham, MD: University Press of America, Inc.

Silverman, S. B., Johnson, R.E., McConnell, N., & Carr, A. (2012, July). Arrogance: A formula for leadership failure. *TIP: The Industrial-Organizational Psychologist, 50*(1), 21–28.

Standish, N. G. (2007). Whatever happened to humility?: Rediscovering a misunderstood leadership strength. *Congregations, 33*(2), 22–26.

Strong, J. (2011). Sitting on the seat of God: A study of pride and hubris in the prophetic corpus of the Hebrew Bible. *Biblical Research, 56,* 55–81.

Su, A., & Wilkins, M. (2013). *Own the room: Discover your signature voice to master your leadership presence.* Boston, MA: Harvard Business Press.

Thoroughgood, C. N., Padilla, A., Hunter, S. T., & Tate, B. W. (2012). The susceptible circle: A taxonomy of followers associated with destructive leadership. *The Leadership Quarterly, 23*(5), 897–917.

de Unamuno, M. (1925). *Essays and soliloquies.* Binghamton, NY: Vail-Ballou Press.

de Unamuno, M. (1954). *Tragic sense of life.* New York, NY: Dover Publications, Inc.

Waldman, D. A., & Bowen, D. E. (2016). Learning to be a paradox-savvy leader. *Academy of Management Perspectives, 30*(3), 316–327.

Welter, B. (2014). *Yesterday's News.* September 3, 1901: Roosevelt 'Big Stick' speech at State Fair. [Blog Post] Retrieved from http://www.startribune.com/sept-3-1901-roosevelt-big-stick-speech-at-state-fair/273586721/

4 Leading through reading and storytelling

Leaders are sensemakers. They set and manage expectations with their rhetoric and stories. Good literature equips leaders with enduring and endearing sets of expectations that both inform and inspire good stories in and out of the workplace. This chapter explores how successful leaders as readers and storytellers have transformed and developed high-performing organizations. This chapter illustrates that people rally around compelling stories to embrace the organizational vision and mission, streamline work priorities, and legitimize their loyalty to the collective. The chapter provides principles and tactics for leaders to craft and communicate sensemaking stories that will help their organizations thrive.

On November 19, 1863, 15,000 people crowded a farm field to hear what would become one of the greatest speeches in American history. While the people came to listen to Edward Everett, the noted orator of the time, it was the relatively last-minute invitee to the platform whose words are most remembered. The keynote speaker would deliver a well-received two-hour speech that consisted of over 13,000 words. The second speaker was asked to provide "a few appropriate remarks"[1] at the conclusion of the inauguration of the National Cemetery at Gettysburg, Pennsylvania. President Abraham Lincoln delivered one of the more profound and recognized speeches in America history in his culturally content-rich and engagingly cadent 272-word Gettysburg Address.

In a letter dated the day after the Address, Edward Everett wrote the following to President Lincoln:

> Permit me also to express my great admiration of the thoughts expressed by you, with such eloquent sensibility & appropriateness, at the consecration of the Cemetery. I should be glad, if I could flatter myself that I came as near the central idea of the occasion in two hours, as you did in two minutes.[2]

The Gettysburg Address by Abraham Lincoln contained three research-proven elements of good pep talks, which Lincoln provided the nation at the dedication of the Federal cemetery. The research on motivating language documented that inspiring and mobilizing speeches provide direction, use empathetic language, and are filled with deeper meaning (McGinn, 2017). In only 272 words, Lincoln provided direction to the nation by connecting the liberty conceived by the founding fathers with the nation's present struggle and the unrealized future when all people would be free and treated as equals. Lincoln empathized with the audience and nation by honoring the dignity of the living and the dead who struggled at the battle. The speech provided a deeper meaning by dedicating the living to the unfinished work of freedom and the longevity of the US democracy.

A story behind the story of the Gettysburg Address was Lincoln's deep knowledge of literature, especially the *Bible*, thus reaffirming the value of being well read in classical literature as a resource for demonstrating exemplary leadership.[3] Elmore (2009) documented that the Gettysburg Address

> is steeped in the words and metaphors of the *King James Bible* and the *Book of Common Prayer*, interspersed with illuminating glances into other works such as the Declaration of Independence and the plays of Shakespeare. It consciously invokes these great works time and again. It shows their beautiful old truths in the rich, sad light of 1863. It transforms their lovely old language into something as close to classical perfection as any public speech has ever achieved. . . . Lincoln. . . was a constant borrower who transformed whatever he took from his constant reading of other writers into strikingly new shapes and meanings.
>
> (pp. 2–3)

Dreisbach (2015) demonstrated that Lincoln's intimate knowledge of the *Bible* provided a deep level of understanding that enabled him to cleverly craft and nobly deliver the Gettysburg Address. Absent such knowledge, the Gettysburg Address might have just been another footnote in history.

> Commentators have long observed that Lincoln drew on diverse literary sources in the Gettysburg Address, among them The *Book of Common Prayer*, the works of Shakespeare, and the *King James Bible*. The most readily apparent of those sources, it would seem, is the *Jacobean Bible*. That said, Lincoln never quoted directly from the *Bible* in his brief address. Yet it is difficult to escape the conclusion that he deliberately invoked biblical intonations, idioms, and themes for rhetorical effect. More important than the use of biblical phrases and cadences was the provocative theme that subtly suggested that those who "gave

their lives" on Gettysburg's battlefield died so the nation might be born again rededicated to the "proposition that all men are created equal," just as Jesus Christ's atoning death on the cross made possible new life for fallen mankind. Lincoln's use of sacred language and themes set a tone of solemnity, emphasized the moral gravity of the message, and infused the great sacrifice of the dead and wounded with profound significance. Moreover, this rhetoric brought comfort and, perhaps, a prophetic voice to a people in the midst of a devastating conflict.

(p. 38)

Books like Gary Wills's (2006), *Lincoln at Gettysburg: The Words That Remade America*; Boritt's (2008), *The Gettysburg Gospel: The Lincoln Speech that Nobody Knows*; and Peatman's (2013), *The Long Shadow of Lincoln's Gettysburg Address*, document how the endearing funeral oratory provided an enduring influence in American history and culture and inspiration for so many other countries. President Lincoln and the Gettysburg Address would be referenced by multiple US presidents and national leaders as the exemplar for free and responsible government and came to represent "the very core of the American creed" (Peatman, 2013). Each organization would do well to have its equivalent of a Gettysburg message that conveys the mission such that it solicits a visceral response, seamlessly connects the heroic past to the uncertain future, shapes high and noble expectations, and honors people and principles.

Unfortunately, many organizational mission statements are void of evocative culturally connected narratives and are distilled to a series of bulleted talking points. Peter Norvig[4] creatively illustrated how uninspiring the Gettysburg Address might look in a modern-day PowerPoint presentation, the primary communication tool for sharing information in organizational and institutional settings. Norvig demonstrated that PowerPoint presentations can neuter the message by attending only to the facts and not the imaginations and experiences of the audience. Traditional messaging targets the mind while rich narrative connecting language moves the head and the heart.

While many organizations may not have an epic story on par with the context of the Gettysburg Address, they do have their own set of dramas that align with the zeitgeist and can provide an engaging sensemaking narrative to their internal and external stakeholders. At minimum, each organization has its own plot with multiple subplots, at different stages of a narrative – a beginning, middle (i.e., a challenge or struggle) and an ending (resolution) that can be leveraged to craft empathetic, meaning making, and direction setting organizational narratives.

Stories of organizations with enviable work cultures abound. Unfortunately, the backstory is often lost when a level of success is achieved. It is easy to think that Nike, Coca-Cola, Google, Apple, FedEx, Starbucks, and McDonalds were always successful and among the most recognizable brands. The back-story is that the founders of such companies started out as young Davids amidst a jungle of other Davids and Goliaths.[5] While many factors facilitated their respective rise to the top, a common denominator is that while the progenitors of such companies created a valuable product, they also crafted a story that resonated with the people, places, and time to establish market share, if for nothing else but to distinguish themselves from their competitors.

This book set out to make the case that literature informs good leader-ship. This thesis does not imply that all good leaders are well read or that readers of good literature will automatically be good leaders or managers. The book advocates that being well read at least positions one to be a better leader for reasons stated in Chapter 1 and illustrated in Chapter 3. As noted in the preface, Harry Truman, an avid reader himself from an early age, wrote that "Readers of good books, particularly books of biography and history, are preparing themselves for leadership. Not all readers become leaders. But all leaders must be readers."

As established in Chapter 1, well-read leaders and managers are posi-tioned to have a deeper reservoir of understanding to not only implement insightful and empathetic habits but also orchestrate organizational mis-sion and management practices into stories that connect and sell. Good literature such as *Don Quixote, Moby-Dick,* and *Pride and Prejudice* not only inform what makes for good leadership, but for the purposes of this chapter, also informs what makes for a good story.

This chapter highlights that a compelling narrative facilitates a strong internal esprit de corps and organizational success. The crafting and telling of endearing and enduring organizational stories elicits purpose and solicits employee engagement above and beyond levels found at organizations where such stories are lacking or are merely utilitarian in nature. A powerfully illustrative example of the role of sensemaking in organizational success is the creation of the National Aeronautics and Space Administration (NASA) and landing the first man on the moon. NASA was urgently founded by an act of Congress in 1958 "to provide for research into problems of flight within and outside the earth's atmosphere, and for other purposes."[6]

The impetus for NASA and the urgency for being the first country to send a man to the moon was the result of an event that transpired on October 4, 1957. *Life Magazine* at the time would describe that event as a "feat that shook the earth."[7] Stephen Bates (1997), writing for *American Heritage* on the 40th anniversary of Sputnik, summarized the details.

> At 6:30 P.M. EST the Associated Press moved a bulletin: Moscow Radio had announced that "the Soviet Union has launched an earth satellite." Later in the evening NBC interrupted regular programming

to give more details of the "man-made moon" and to play its high-pitched radio signal "as recorded by RCA engineers." The next morning's New York Times and Washington Post both gave three-line eight-column banners to the feat, the kind of headline reserved for a Pearl Harbor or a D-Day. The editors of Newsweek scrapped their planned feature on Detroit's new line of cars (trashing 1,309,990 cover copies—twenty tons of paper). The new cover showed an artist's conception of the Soviet satellite Sputnik (Russian for "fellow traveler"). Inside, the weekly explained "The Red Conquest, "The Meaning to the World," and, ominously, "Why We Are Lagging."

OVERNIGHT THE self-assured center began coming apart. Inventive, free enterprise America, home of Edison and the Wright brothers, Levittown and "modern labor saving kitchen appliances," was being overtaken—surpassed?—by a backward, totalitarian, Communist nation. And the shock to can-do pride was the least of it. A missile gap apparently yawned, with the Soviets pulling decisively ahead in the ultimate nuclear weapons, ICBMs. Democrats in Congress charged that amiable Ike's mid-register budgetary caution had jeopardized U.S. military prowess. It seemed that the energetic five-star architect of victory in the Big War had turned into a Burning Tree Country Club slacker (one cartoonist showed Sputnik whizzing past a golf ball), a myopic Pangloss, a President Magoo.[8]

US citizens were already scared about the threat of nuclear war between the Soviet Union and the United States but took some solace that their perceived technical and moral superiority would make them the ultimate winners in the space and arms races. But when a Russian made basketball-sized object orbited the United States to be the first man-made satellite in space, any hopes of winning the cold war were temporarily dashed. Americans were put on high alert, at least for the next 12 years until Neil Armstrong and Buzz Aldrin would land the lunar module Eagle on the moon on July 20, 1969. Within months of Sputnik, the US Congress drafted legislation to establish NASA with the goal of winning the space race. Once the National Aeronautical Space Act was signed into law by President Eisenhower on July 29, 1958, America entered the space race with a new zeal and focus with the ultimate goal to protect the general welfare and security of the United States and the rest of the world from the looming threat of communism propagated by the aggressive Soviet Union under premier Nikita Khrushchev.

NASA in 1958 was tasked with three open-ended goals: improve space technology to meet national interests in space, achieve preeminence in space for the United States, and advance science by exploring the solar system (National Aeronautics and Space Act, 1958). While the goals were ambitious, they were too open-ended to provide a clear focus by which the nation, Congress, and NASA personnel could rally around. The United States would suffer another psychological blow more alarming than Sputnik on April 12, 1961 when Soviet cosmonaut Yuri Gagarin became the first person to orbit the earth. It was then when President Kennedy gave NASA a very specific goal that would focus with laser precision the work in NASA and establish an unprecedented esprit de corps among a peak of 420,000 people working directly or indirectly with NASA in the Apollo era (Levine, 1982).

The JFK Library described what President Kennedy did next.

> President Kennedy understood the need to restore America's confidence and intended not merely to match the Soviets, but surpass them. On May 25, 1961, he stood before Congress to deliver a special message on "urgent national needs." He asked for an additional $7 billion to $9 billion over the next five years for the space program, proclaiming that "this nation should commit itself to achieving the goal, before the decade is out, of landing a man on the moon and returning him safely to the earth." President Kennedy settled upon this dramatic goal as a means of focusing and mobilizing the nation's lagging space efforts.[9]

By establishing a compelling and concrete mission that encapsulated the ambitions and hopes of the nation, Kennedy transformed the 1960s work culture at NASA where people across all levels of the organization became obsessed with getting a man to the moon (Carton, 2018). By providing a rallying point around an emotional narrative, Kennedy worked with NASA to help employees connect their day-to-day activities and specific goals to the urgent near-future objective, such that there were unprecedented levels of engagement and excitement for those working with and for NASA between 1961 and 1969 when the first US astronauts landed on the moon (Carton, 2018).

The levels of employee engagement were so high during NASA's heyday that the following apocryphal story emerged to capture the mood of the time and was consistently repeated to remind people associated with NASA why their best efforts mattered and were needed. The story goes that President John F. Kennedy was touring NASA one night when he came upon a custodian mopping the floors. When Kennedy asked the employee why he was working so late, the custodian responded, "Because I am not mopping the floors, I'm putting a man on the moon" (Carton, 2018, p. 354).[10]

Simon (1964) shared a similar illustration of a bricklayer in documenting the power of the narrative to mediate between what Simon described as a "divorce between personal goals and organizational roles" in the work setting which often manifests itself in lower levels of employee engagement (p. 14). Simon used three interpretations to describe the work of a bricklayer as that of laying bricks, building a wall, or building a cathedral. The latter interpretation keeps the ultimate end in sight and gives meaning beyond that of just building a wall. Simon demonstrated that organizational goal(s) are "modified by managers and employees at all echelons" (p. 2) because people have multiple roles and responsibilities (i.e., loyalties to other narratives and psychological contracts). As a result, formal organizational goals may or may not coincide with employees' informal goals. It is sensemaking or perspective-taking that determines when one internalizes his or her organizational role and demonstrates higher levels of engagement like the NASA custodian or the bricklayer claiming that he is building a cathedral rather than just laying bricks or building a wall.

It is worth underscoring that Kennedy, like Lincoln, was an avid reader from an early age. *Life Magazine* called President JFK the US First Reader in an article titled, "The President's Voracious Reading Habits: He Eats up News, Books at 1,200 Words a Minute." The author of the article, Hugh Sidey (1961), noted that JFK "caused a revolution in the reading habits of his staff members" (p. 55) just so they could keep up with him. Sidey relayed a conversation between James McGregor Burns, author of *John Kennedy: A Political Profile,* and JFK that took place in a Wisconsin restaurant in 1960 while on the campaign trail. JFK asked Burns what he had been reading lately which led to a conversation which revealed that "Kennedy had read more of the books discussed than Professor Burns" (p. 59). Sidey noted that "The significance of reading is best summarized by the President himself. Not long ago he said to Burns, 'Roosevelt got most of his ideas from talking to people. I get most of mine from reading" (p. 59).

JFK's curious intellect, like Lincoln's, equipped him to skillfully incorporate elevated language in his writings and speeches, especially in his inaugural speech that, like the Gettysburg Address, used culturally loaded words to connect listeners to their noble past and destiny to become one of America's greatest speeches.[11] His precision with words even mattered for his memos. Sidey (1961) noted that JFK considered "memo-writing an important governmental art" and that he took "great pains with the memos" that he sent to his departments (p. 60). Kennedy knew that leading and governing was about sensemaking and that good sensemaking came from reading deeply and broadly.

Karl Weick (1995) legitimized the formal study of leaders as sensemakers as a part of organizational studies with his seminal book, *Sensemaking in Organizations*. He posited that while most managers exclusively utilize logical argumentation and persuasion to get the work done, "most organizational realities are based upon narration" (p. 127). Weick basically argued that sensemaking activities abound in organizations to deal with identity, complexity, and ambiguity and that leaders and managers would do well to shape the narrative as much as possible to align core values with organizational practices. He demonstrated that stories shape vocabularies and experiences and that the choice of words and narrative matter. Weick (1995) stated that

> rich vocabularies matter in a world of action where images of actions rather than the actions themselves are passed from person to person. Rich vocabularies give options for construing the meaning of action and are more likely to reveal latent opportunities.
>
> (pp. 183–184)

Hutchinson (2018), Maitlis and Christianson (2014), Forman (2013), Denning (2011), Schein (2010), and Guber (2007) reinforced Weick's conclusions that work cultures are created and maintained by the narratives people use to give meaning to what and why they do what they do. Bolman and Deal (2013) in their seminal book, *Reframing Organizations*, documented four dominant narratives that exist in organizations. The structural, human relations, political, and symbolic frameworks are equally at play throughout organizations, but when leaders limit themselves to one narrative, they fail to optimize their impact. Bolman and Deal underscored the importance of taking on multiple frames to be effective leaders. For Bolman and Deal, much of symbolic leadership involves sensemaking in the form storytelling.

The following case studies of thriving businesses illustrate the connections among leaders' literacy in non-business literature, sensemaking activities, and organizational success.

Case 1

This first case study is a collective story of four leaders in the manufacturing business and their corresponding companies. The four leaders were interviewed exclusively for this chapter and were asked about their reading habits, the stories they tell, and if they perceived a connection to their business success. Each of the leaders acknowledged that they read extensively and have stories that define their values and guide their business practices.

Their commonalities are just as profound as their differences. The four businesses are located in Winona, Minnesota, a small town on the Mississippi River.[12] The four leaders grew up in Minnesota, three of whom were born in Winona. Of the leaders, two were founders, one was the grandson of the founder, and the fourth the long-term owner. Each company has been in business for at least 50 years. They are multi-million-dollar companies, one of which is a billion-dollar company.

While similar, the four companies have substantive differences. The one publicly held company of the four is the largest fastener distributor in North America with over 20,000 employees. The other manufacturing companies are privately held. One is a global reinforced thermoplastics manufacturer and leader in customized engineered plastic compounds with over 1,300 employees. The third is a leading manufacturer of licensed promotional products for retailers, professional sport teams, concessionaires, colleges, and businesses, distributors, and schools with over 650 employees. The fourth is the leading producer of high-end custom canoes with 100 employees. Fastenal, founded in 1967 has over $4.5 billion in sales. RTP, officially founded in 1982 was part of the family plastics business in 1948 with roots to the original family business from the early 1920s, generates over $650 million in annual sales. Wincraft, founded in 1961, yields over $100 million in sales. Wenonah Canoes, founded in 1967, is a hobby business generating around $15 million dollars in sales.

In addition to very different products, the leaders had different educational backgrounds. Bob Kierlin, the founder of Fastenal, earned a BS in Engineering and MBA from the University of Minnesota. Hugh Miller, CEO of RTP, earned a BA in Political Science from Northwestern University. Dick Pope, Chairman of Wincraft earned a BA in Economics and minor in philosophy at Saint John's University in Minnesota (a Catholic liberal arts college). Mike Cichanowski, founder and CEO of Wenonah Canoe, attended Winona State University but started his business in lieu of finishing his degree.

When it came to reading, all four were extensive readers with varying reading lists and habits throughout their life. Hugh Miller stated that when he was younger, he read several books a week, primarily history and spy books. He also shared that on long business trips to and from Asia that he would purposely read books that he would not normally read, just to learn new things and think differently.

Mike Cichanowski provided his standard reading list of 20 trade journals, periodicals, and newspapers that occupy approximately 1.5 hours of his time most mornings prior to going to his manufacturing facility. An avid reader and an advocate of reading from both political spectrums, Mike shared that he found the trade journals filled with "good stuff" that helped him be an eclectic leader. Dick Pope has an extensive library in his office and home with readings primarily related to sports and business, given his company is primarily in the business of sports. His books are predominately on successful coaches like Vince Lombardi and John Wooden and successful businesses like the Mayo Clinic, Fastenal, NFL, and Walmart and their respective founders.

Bob Kierlin shared that the most significant book in his life was a copy of *Tom Sawyer* that he received as a Christmas gift from his aunt and uncle when he was seven years old. It meant something to him at that time to have a real book to read. While serving in the Peace Corps in South America, in an age and location where books were hard to come by, Bob read a copy of *Don Quixote* in Spanish and regularly read via mail subscription *The New Yorker, Saturday Review of Literature,* and the *New York Review of Books.* Bob was also familiar with a classic, but somewhat obscure, book in the humanities, *Mont Saint Michel and Chartres,* by esteemed historian Henry Adams.[13] Bob, in one of his writings, stated that

> My understanding of what is called Gross Domestic Product did not come from economics classes as much as it did from Henry Adam's book, "*Mont St. Michel and Chartres*". This book talks about the Great European cathedrals and the people who built them. For a period of approximately 100 years, about three large churches or cathedrals were completed each year.
>
> The effort represented about 35% of the estimated Gross Domestic Product of these people.
>
> (Kierlin, 1993, p. 29)

Bob also shared that when he worked at IBM prior to launching Fastenal he took advantage of the IBM library and picked up much by reading different magazines and books. An interesting vignette of Bob's sense of literature is captured in a conversation that he had with his high school buddy Julius Gernes who went to Saint Mary's University of Minnesota to pursue a BA in Liberal Arts. Bob asked Julius why he was "wasting his money on that degree when he could get that at the public library?" While Julius was able to defend his degree choice and would eventually become a lawyer representing the County of Winona, Bob did admit to reading many theatrical plays to keep up with his friend, thereby indirectly pursuing his own study in the liberal arts.

While immersed in the readings associated with their respective industries, especially in the early stages of their business careers, all four business leaders shared that their eclectic readings outside the business genre made them more open-minded in their outlooks, cultivated an appreciation for people and their differences, equipped them to make connections that might otherwise be missed, provided a sense of what would and would not work, and allowed them to make more holistic decisions. It should be noted that making explicit business connections from their reading habits and history was a bit like asking a fish to describe water. It just seemed natural to internalize what was read and glean useful principles for leading and managing. Instead of getting comments about specific books and corresponding business practices, the comments were more general, about cultivating an eclectic or more aesthetic elements of good leadership and practices.

The learning from the readings became internalized and could not but help leak out when needed, especially in crafting their respective stories. Mike Cichanowski stated that the outside readings probably cultivated his intuition. Dick Pope shared that a broad background of knowledge such as music and theatre allows one to connect with people and build relationships, a necessary ingredient for sustaining a successful business. The sense from the interviews is that extensive reading provided a deep well of understanding to make associations, cultivate habits of the heart that otherwise would have been missed, and informed what was necessary to develop and sustain profitable and well-regarded companies by employees, customers, and competitors.

It is worth noting that three of the leaders referenced that the demand on time focused what and when they read. For example, in the early start-up stage, the technical and trade journals occupied their attention. Formal education exposed them to different aspects of the humanities, including various works of great literature. Bob Kierlin noted that life can be simply divided into three phases: (1) learning to do things, (2) doing things, and (3) resting after doing things (Kierlin, 1993, p. 28). It is phase one and three that people can strategically take time to judiciously read the classics and benefit from the wisdom thereof.

Three leaders reported that they had stories they consistently "preached" so as to enthuse values in and throughout their respective companies. Since the four companies deal with manufacturing, their signature stories center on customer service and commitment to consistently providing products of the highest quality. As Dick Pope noted, in manufacturing, the message is simple, "it gets down to quality and service." Obviously, a good story starts with a quality product, but a product without a compelling story and service will not make for a successful business. Mike Cichanowski stated that it is easy to make stuff, but it is more difficult to sell stuff. He described that there are many good craftsmen out there, but they go unnoticed because they don't know how to sell their product.[14]

Hugh Miller reported that he is consistently telling stories of exemplary customer service, quality, and integrity to colleagues and customers, a point reiterated by his administrative assistant. Hugh was adamant that products would not be shipped unless they met all the specifications, noting that some competitors might cheat on the standards or lie, but integrity was a nonnegotiable at RTP. At RTP, sales engineers are "quarterbacks for the customers, in that they call the shots to make sure that the customers receive flawless products according to their specifications." The quarterback metaphor and corresponding examples told frequently within the company gives meaning to RTP's quality policy,

> Through the continual improvement of our quality system, processes and products, RTP Company is committed to the delivery of on-time, defect-free products which meet or exceed the requirements of our internal and external customers.

Bob Kierlin shared one signature story that captured the company's core values and served as a point of reference for shaping organizational culture. Awhile back in the early days of Fastenal, a manager at a Ford plastics plant in Indiana called a local Fastenal store manager for some metric bolt fasteners for an emergency job. The original supplier needed a week to customize and ship the replacement fasteners, hence rendering the plant inoperative and disrupting the supply chain and lives of employees. While not an official vendor for the Ford plant, the Fastenal store manager called the Fastenal manufacturing plant supervisor in Winona on Friday to initiate a rush order. Through creative maneuvering, they secured blank fasteners, cut them down to the needed metric, had them hardened, and then chartered a plane to deliver them in Indiana so that they could be installed that Sunday night, saving the Ford plant hundreds of thousands of dollars. The story reflects Bob's philosophy and ability to empower all Fastenal employees to grow the company through customer service and internalize the company's core values of ambition, innovation, integrity, and teamwork.

When asked how often Bob gets to share that story and similar stories to engage employees, create customer loyalty, and establish market share, Bob said ironically that he put the stories in a book, *The Power of Fastenal People* (Kierlin, 2015), to be a teaching tool for Fastenal leaders. The book is available to Fastenal managers and is an insightful read that reflects the wisdom behind its success. The book has three subtitles:

1   Why Do Some Companies Thrive... While Other Companies Just Survive?

2   The Teamwork Approach to Everyday Problem-Solving for Reaching Practicable, Common Goal Solutions.

3   Here's a First-Hand Account of the FASTENAL COMPANY Leadership Principles at Work in the Workplace... and Beyond.

The Power of Fastenal People is a good read on the Fastenal culture and expectations, and, quite candidly, a good read for leaders and managers in any company as it incorporates timeless principles and insight not often captured in traditional business books. It seems prudent that all companies should have a must read that captures their core values in stories that illustrate and model expectations.

The power of stories is probably best illustrated in Wincraft's success. Wincraft makes non-athletic apparel memorabilia for sport teams, colleges and schools, and businesses. Dick Pope noted that people want to be associated with winners and therefore will purchase products such as banners, decals, drinkware, jewelry, pens and pencils, pennants, towels, and umbrellas that connect them with their favorite team, school, and organization. He noted that when people's favorite teams are winning, they will often say "we are winning." He shared that attitudes are just different when people are associated with a winning organization, noting as an example that when colleges have winning teams, recruitment and fundraising go up. He created a company that capitalizes on people's need and desire for affinity and identification with something bigger than themselves (i.e., a good story).

It appears from this collective case study that there are two types of storytelling in the manufacturing world. Stories about the product itself, its niche and quality, and stories about customer service. Such stories abound in all four companies but were especially evident in Wenonah Canoes's narrative. Their promotional literature reveals that expert craftsmen combine "soul with science" to provide freedom, adventure, and a state of mind by selling high-end canoes, kayaks, and stand-up paddle boards. Mike even tells the Wenonah story with an assortment of artistic tin signs to promote his canoes and the canoeing experience.

A noteworthy feature of the leaders is their connection to their community and corresponding philanthropic endeavors. These include the Miller Mentoring, Morrie Miller Athletic Foundation, Ben & Adith Miller Patient Care Fund, and the Minnesota Beethoven Festival[15] associated with Hugh Miller and RTP and the Hiawatha Education Foundation and the Minnesota Maritime Museum[16] associated with Bob Kierlin and Fastenal. The small river community of 27,000 residents is home to an art museum and classical musical festival on par with those found in major cities, thanks to the enlightened perspectives of their respective benefactors.

The combined case study of the four successful business leaders and their thriving companies suggests a connection that the more managers read in and outside the business literature, the more enlightened their business models, practices, and corporate narratives. Obviously, it requires much sweat equity to create and sustain a successful business, or as Dick Pope noted, "leaders have to live their business, feel it, see it, make decisions by being close to it." But there is something unique at work when entrepreneurs can start and sustain a business for 50 plus years given the low survival rate for businesses.[17] While there are equally successful business people who are not as well read as Bob Kierlin, Hugh Miller, Dick Pope, and Mike Cichanowski, it is fair to say their formal and informal education provided tacit ways of thinking, talking, and doing that gave them a competitive edge to be respected and successful leaders in the Winona community and their respective industries.

Case 2

The second case study is a series of vignettes from the research on organizational storytelling conducted over four years by Dr. Janis Forman, the founder and Director of the Management Communication Program at the UCLA Anderson School of Management. Dr. Forman, who happens to hold a doctorate in comparative literature, interviewed over 140 people representing approximately 50 organizations. She provided compelling insights on the use of stories and organizational identity from her field research at Chevron, FedEx, Schering-Plough, and Philips. She documented how authentic storytelling connected people with organizational core values and activities beyond what traditional business speak typically accomplished. Her book, *Storytelling in Business: The Authentic and Fluent Organization* provided research-based descriptions, examples, and evidence for leaders and managers to be *listening storytellers.*

In the opening chapters, Forman (2013) used *craft* as a noun and verb to provide guidelines for "making good choices about a variety of story elements" found in "every successful film, short story, and novel" (p. 50). The process involves a clear purpose, knowledge of the audience, relevant details that evoke the five senses, compelling language, and a narrative logic. The remaining chapters examined in detail how four companies successfully developed and implemented different storytelling activities to both reflect and create transformational social realities consistent with their respective values, mission, and vision.

Forman (2013) cogently demonstrated that successful businesses listen to and sell stories more than they sell products and services, with the Philips story the most compelling example. Philips was founded in 1891 as a light bulb manufacturer to become a leader in professional healthcare and consumer health with almost 74,000 employees and EUR 17.8 billion in sales at the end of 2017. Philips was dominating the consumer electronics market, when CEO Gerard Kliesterlee observed in 2001 that

> the electronic components for which the company was known were fast becoming a commodity business. As a result, the company would need to shift its strategic direction and then develop the appropriate branding to communicate the shift and inspire internal and external stakeholders alike to embrace the benefits of the change and implications.
>
> (pp. 159–160)

At this point, Philips reframed its "focus on helping people have better lives, what Philips calls "health and well-being" (Forman, 2013, p. 160). As Philips was rebranding itself, Kliesterlee observed that people throughout the company had different versions of the Philips story and tended to focus on the technical product specifications, useful, albeit limiting. To get everyone (not just those in marketing) on the same script was a challenge in a "culture dominated by engineers and in an organization that was a conglomerate of ten to fifteen acquisitions, and had five business units and sales and services in one hundred countries" (Forman, 2013, p. 161). Philips initiated storytelling workshops across the organization to address the challenge of getting Philips' internal stakeholders to think and act differently.

The new Philips story and storytelling workshops positioned the company to be a solutions-seeking company, take the lead in innovation in their targeted sectors, shift from a technology-centric to a people-centered approach, and capture the market share for their various products. Forman (2013) tells the story of one business-minded manager in Philips' Lighting who was reluctant to embrace the new story gathering and telling model. He was "used to speaking to customers in terms of numbers and products" and now uses "art books full of magnificent photos of cityscapes and famous architectural sights illuminated and transformed by lighting" (p. 192).

Forman (2013) included a quote from a VP of Corporate Communications with Philips Lighting that captured the value and nature of storytelling and storytelling workshops that allowed the company to shift from a "technology-centric to a people-centric approach to the market" and "move from lumen to human" (p. 158).

> Before the workshops, company communication was much more about broadcasting functional messages about technology, about semiconductors, lumens per watt, ballast and bulbs. Our people were not thinking about how our technology could really help people's lives.
>
> (p. 158)

The use of storytelling changed the ethos at Philips Lighting from "lighting a desk" to creating a "desired social space," unbounding one's rationality,[18] and igniting innovative growth mindsets.

Schering-Plough implemented a similar strategy and tactic to confront recent legal and market challenges that warranted a set of corrective actions. At the time of the Forman's case study, Schering-Plough was a global healthcare company with 50,000 employees. In April 2003, on his third day as the new CEO and chairman, Fred Hassan outlined a "six-to-eight-year journey of transformation from being in severe stress to high performance" (p. 55). Hassan described Shering-Plough as a "wounded company in prolonged decline... but one that can be turned around" (p. 55). He advocated a slow, steady, and manageable approach in an Action Agenda that had five "chapters." Forman (2013) reported that "on his fourth day at the company, Hassan announced the story in chapters to employees in a town-hall meeting, which was video broadcast, taped, and rebroadcast" (p. 56). The five chapters were titled *stabilize, repair, turn around, build the base, and breakout.* Hassan methodically implemented his plans in stages and kept sharing the meta-narrative of his Action Agenda, emphasizing core values, and providing examples of heroes in the company at regular and frequent town-hall meetings. As the final chapter, *break out*, was being implemented in Schering-Plough's turn around, "an alternative ending" emerged (p. 65) when in 2009 Merck acquired Schering-Plough for $41 billion.

Hassan's chapter stories in his *Action Agenda* served as reference points to mark and measure success at the predetermined intervals. His frequent retelling of the story with updates created opportunities for others to internalize the story, sustained a positive rumor mill, and allowed people to remain focused on the human outcomes through the various growing pains. It is worth noting that the human stories by themselves were insufficient. As evidenced by Schering-Plough's turnaround, the stories must be authentic in that they mirror the organizational core values and activities and the leaders' behaviors and vice versa. The stories must also include hard data as proof points if the stories are to have credibility and staying power. In other words, the stories must live up to their claims and must include a judicious amount of corroborating evidence. Unfortunately, many businesses remain relatively sterile with sound numbers but no endearing or compelling story to give the bottom-line numbers transcendent meaning.

The FedEx culture of storytelling documented by Forman is the third and final vignette for this chapter. FedEx is a global transportation company with 425,000 team members and $65.5 billion in revenue for 2018 fiscal year. Fred Smith wrote a paper for his economics course at Yale that outlined the new market for overnight delivery which became the impetus for him starting FedEx in 1971. An interesting story of Fred Smith's unorthodox business savvy from the early days was when he parlayed FedEx's last $5,000 to $27,000 at Blackjack in Las Vegas to cover a $24,000 fuel bill to let FedEx operate until financing was secured for the new company.

FedEx has been a storytelling company since its early years. According to Forman (2013), in 1988, Fred Smith initiated in-house corporate television channels to facilitate open communication. He provided quarterly reports on FXTV, daily news updates, and regular video highlights of employees' achievements. By 2002, FXTV was connected to 2000 sites. Forman noted that although those "technological capabilities may seem ordinary by today's standards, they were then state-of-the-art for corporate America" (p. 128).

In 2005, FedEx hired a former senior producer at MSNBC and ABC to reinvent FXTV with the latest technology and transition from its traditional news reporting approach to a "journalistic approach to employee engagement: character-driven stories that informed through emotive narrative" (p. 129). Diane Terrell, Managing Director of Global Broadcast and Interactive Communications, noted the "new media technology dominated every conversation" and eliminated "the traditional avenues" of communicating updates and managing change associated with growth (p. 129). Soon communications joined forces with marketing to leverage social media to be a listening company and in 2009 created a Digital and Social Media Engagement team to modernize the FedEx business culture by "encouraging higher degrees of collaboration, participations, and engagement through social media strategies" (p. 130).

Forman (2013) asked, why the emphasis on stories at FedEx, particularly digital stories? While several themes emerged, "digital storytelling would take a dominant position in communications to bridge the divides of a workforce that is 'global, multicultural, and multilingual'" so as to "create a 'shared global experience that is not solely dependent on language'" (p. 131). According to Forman, the collection and sharing of FedEx stories served to:

- Highlight customer experiences and document that the company "does more than move packages. It has a higher calling in terms of increasing the standard of living and quality of life" (p. 132).
- Promote and reinforce the company's brand and reputation.
- Display the company's thought leadership.

Forman cited an executive with FedEx when describing the role of stories,

> FedEx has built its culture in part around heroic stories, the enormous lengths to which employees will go to deliver "golden packages,"

such as a FedEx truck driver who pulled an elderly man out of his car in a flood, or a team of employees who successfully delivered 90 tons of artifacts from the *Titanic* destined for an exhibition in Atlanta but stranded in southern Italy. Stories of these discretionary efforts by employees who have prevailed in the face of substantial obstacles are, Margaritis[19] adds, the centerpiece of communications about culture.

Seeing and hearing heroic stories become self-fulfilling. People are rejuvenated through stories. They hear heroic stories and want to emulate them. You can't legislate the heart, the extra step people will take. No training or rulebook defines whether someone goes above and beyond. No training or rule book can force someone to be loyal or motivated. Employees are our ambassadors and represent and promote the company.

(pp. 133–134)

Forman's thorough and recent research demonstrated that organizations would do well to adopt storytelling practices to create and sustain thriving and competitive organizational cultures. Philips used storytelling workshops to transform its culture to become a global innovative solutions provider. Schering-Plough used an *Action Agenda* storyboard to engage in turn-around change. FedEx initiated storytelling platforms and culture to promote its core values.

The craft of storytelling

Leaders and managers are storytellers. As the official organizational narrators, they shape the formal and informal work place stories by what they say (and don't say) and do (and don't do). While the remaining pages cannot do justice in describing what is required to be skilled raconteurs, they provide some basic principles and tactics on the art and science of storytelling and highlight why storytelling should be a part of every leader's repertoire. A premise of this book is that reading great works of literature is a solid starting point. Connoisseurs of good stories cannot but help glean the elements and content necessary to craft engaging and endearing work stories.

Stephen Denning is a leading advocate for leading and managing with storytelling. It was his work at the World Bank in the mid-1990s as a manager that made Denning realize that discourse beyond "rates of return, cost-benefit analyses, risk assessment, performance targets, budget, work programs, the bottom line – you name it," although important, did not provide a tipping point for timely innovation at the World Bank (Denning, 2011, p. 1). It was then that Denning experienced an epiphany.

> I was facing a leadership challenge for which the traditional tools of management were impotent. In trying to communicate a new idea to a skeptical audience, I found that the virtues of sharpness and rigor were not working. Having spent my life believing in the dream of reason, I was startled to find that an appropriately told story had the power to do what rigorous analysis couldn't: to communicate a strange new idea and move people to enthusiastic action.
>
> (p. 2)

Denning continued to reflect on his conversion to storytelling as a core management skill.

> Initially the idea that storytelling might be a powerful tool for management and leadership was so counterintuitive and contrary to my entire education and work-life experience that I had difficulty in believing the evidence of my own eyes. In fact, it took me several years to admit to myself that I was being successful through telling stories.
>
> (p. 2)

Denning's books, *The Secret Language of Leadership: How Leaders Inspire Actions Through Narrative* (2007) and *The Leader's Guide to Radical Management* (2010) documented the value and techniques for business managers and leaders to think, speak, and act differently around well-crafted narratives rather than to rely exclusively on financial incentives and benchmarks to rally internal and external stakeholders. Denning's (2011) *The Leader's Guide to Storytelling: Mastering the Art and Discipline of Business Narrative* was written to provide communication tools for leaders at all levels of an organization to be master storytellers, claiming that "the basics of leadership storytelling can be mastered quickly" while "mastery of the discipline . . . takes a lifetime" as storytelling is a performance art that improves with rehearsals and recitals (p. 11).[20]

After stumbling into business storytelling, Denning would go on to research, consult, and write, on the art and science of storytelling in organizations. Denning (2011) noted that while traditional storytelling has much in common with organizational storytelling, the latter has at least two unique features. In traditional storytelling situations, there is time for the plot to unfold. In business settings, the raconteur has seconds to get to the point. Most stories in other settings such as theatre, television, novels, film, and social gatherings are primarily designed to entertain. Business stories are designed to inform, persuade, or inspire. As a result, crafting and telling stories in organizational settings for business purposes and audiences is more nuanced than just telling stories.

It is worth noting that there are two types of organizational stories. There are scripted and organic stories. The latter involves stories that people develop as a result of a spontaneous experience and share as a result of the moment. The scripted stories are the ones managers carefully craft to accomplish specific objectives. Both types of stories have a cohesive beginning, middle, and end; they evoke emotions and excite additional senses (Dolan & Naidu, 2013). They are told because they capture and communicate a timely point, and reflect and create social realities.

Leaders and managers want to carefully craft stories that become the metanarratives for the organic stories. Accordingly, Denning (2011) identified eight narrative patterns, depending on the business objective(s) for story:

- Ignite action and implement new ideas. Reason alone is not sufficient to cause people to change, hence the power of stories to motivate.
- Communicate who you are. Authentic identity stories about oneself establish transparency, credibility, and trust between the storyteller and audience. Denning makes an important note that people would do well to craft their own narrative, their purpose, which from all other life choices are made.
- Communicate who the company is – branding. The social media world has shifted branding from one-way messaging to a single audience to a two-way communication process to discerning, if not skeptical, consumers. According to Denning, branding must now consist of stories about the business itself (why should consumers and clients go with you?), product or services (quality matters), and the customer (bond and connect with the product and services by identifying with others).
- Transmit values. All businesses have stated and unstated virtues and ethics that drive practices. Stories become values in action and therefore reveal and create organizational cultures.
- Foster collaboration. Stories unite and create an esprit de corps around common values and goals by shaping expectations and norms.
- Tame the grapevine. Stories abound in the workplace and spread effortlessly and fast. Managers let their stories fuel the ubiquitous rumor mill lest others take precedence and counter misleading and/or false stories.
- Share knowledge. Stories give meaning to the details and cultivate a tacit understanding of the knowledge being transmitted.

- Leading people into the future. Stories help people visualize a future beyond what is conveyed in typical vision statements and to think outside the box of their present state of affairs, a necessary element for companies to remain innovative.

Regardless of the type of narrative, Denning (2011) provided four key elements for managers and leaders to tell a "right" story in a "right" way in a business setting: style, truth, preparation, and delivery. Denning encourages organizational storytellers to speak as if they were talking to a single individual. The one-on-one communication style paradoxically allows speakers to connect with everyone in the audience by being themselves and come across as personable and relatable. Good organizational storytellers keep their story simple, clear, and focused lest they lose their audience. In addition, Denning noted that "style isn't something separate from the person or detachable from the content of what is said" (p. 46). In other words, good storytellers are themselves when sharing the story, not a spokesperson. While the story maybe scripted, it is told from a place of conviction because the message has been owned and internalized such that the message and messenger are one. As a result, the storyteller provides a freshness to the script to enhance the legitimacy of both the story and the narrator.

Good storytellers tell the truth of the situation in contrast to stories filled with embellishments or distortions that mislead or deceive. For truth to be a key stylistic feature, the speaker and listeners must be trustworthy. The third element is often the most laborious. Telling the story right takes much preparation and many rehearsals. Writing and rehearsing the story makes the presenter comfortable with the narrative and provides opportunity to massage the message during the multiple dry runs. The rehearsals allow for sound checks (stories have to appeal to the ear), gauge timing (brevity is key), and ongoing refinement of content and mannerism until the message and messenger are in sync. The delivery, the verbal and nonverbal aspects of every message, is the final element. Good delivery requires the storytellers to be comfortable, know their audience, enunciate well, implement gestures, engage in eye contact, maintain good posture and open body stance, and sustain a high level of energy when sharing.

The good news is that people do not need to wait until they are seasoned storytellers to create and share timely organizational stories. While it is a skill that improves with each rehearsal, people are by nature story seekers and makers. People just have to recall how easily they were mesmerized by stories and loved to recount stories as a child to reawaken their natural story making and telling personae.[21]

Summary and conclusion

A valuable education can be found in great literature. Like much of all formal education, continual reading has a cumulative effect. While adults may not recall when they learned their addition and subtraction skills, they know them and use them on a regular basis. Similar to reading fiction and nonfiction, facts and ideas are learned only to become the basis of future learning and thinking. The business leaders in case study one not only evidenced a business savvy but also demonstrated a holistic understanding of people and life that allowed them to develop prosperous companies and philanthropic initiatives. The vignettes referenced in the second case study revealed that dynamic managed storytelling can guide strategic change and promote highly engaged and productive work cultures in ways not realized in traditional management approaches.

Lincoln's Gettysburg Address and John F. Kennedy's focused goal setting with NASA demonstrated the transformational nature of brief narratives that connect, set direction, and provide meaning. The story and work of Denning provided examples and techniques for leaders and managers to craft and deliver their business stories the right way. Attending to style and truth and rehearsing until the story is internalized are all pre-delivery activities. Delivery is more than just recounting; it involves connecting with the audience in a genuine and sincere manner.

People love good stories, and even better, good stories told well. Leaders and managers who develop and implement the craft of storytelling in business have additional tools in their tool belt to optimize the performance of their respective work communities. In addition, they may well find that it is the most effective go-to tool to use to engage and endear internal and external stakeholders.

This chapter and book rightly conclude with a story that clearly demonstrates a link between successful business ventures and books.

In 1848, at the age of 13, Andrew Carnegie relocated to Allegheny Pennsylvania from Dunfermline Scotland with his family. He began work in a factory soon upon his arrival to help his father, mother, and brother gain financial independence from their maternal uncle and aunt who hosted them upon their arrival to the United States. Andrew soon secured a job as a telegraph messenger boy, and by 1853, he was working as the assistant and telegrapher for a top official with the Pennsylvania Railroad Company. It was during this period that Andrew received what he described as a "blessing from above, a means by which the treasures of literature were unfolded" to him (Carnegie, 1920, p. 45).

By way of background, by the age of 30, Andrew Carnegie would go from working in a cotton mill, a telegraph company, and with the

Pennsylvania Railroad to eventually have business interests in rail sleeping cars, iron bridges, railroads, and oil wells. He subsequently established the largest steel manufacturing company in the world. In 1901, at the age of 65, Andrew sold Carnegie Steel to J.P. Morgan for $480 million to become the world's wealthiest person at the time and, even in today's dollars, the equivalent of a staggering $309 billion.[22]

Carnegie would spend the remainder of his life, until he died at the age of 83 in 1919, distributing his wealth consistent with the tenets he outlined in *The Gospel of Wealth* (1900), where he stated that "The man who dies thus rich dies disgraced."[23] Andrew advocated that the wealthy had an obligation to judiciously administer their wealth by developing institutions that would benefit society. The Carnegie Organization lists 15 organizations Andrew endowed, including, but not limited to Carnegie Mellon University, Carnegie Foundation for the Advancement of Teaching, and Carnegie Hall. Andrew Carnegie would establish different pension funds, including what is now known at TIAA-CREF, one of the largest financial services in the world, primarily serving college and university personnel.[24] Carnegie is probably best known for founding 2,509 public libraries around the globe to become the Patron Saint of Libraries, all as a result of his prodigious experience with Colonel James Anderson, who Andrew met during his initial years in the United States.

Colonel James Anderson, who served in the War of 1812, opened his personal library to working boys in the neighborhood. Carnegie was one of the boys who took advantage of the unprecedented opportunity. He would describe in his autobiography the profound impact that access to books would have on his life.

> Books which it would have been impossible for me to obtain elsewhere were, by his wise generosity, placed within my reach; and to him I owe a taste for literature which I would not exchange for all the millions that were ever amassed by man. Life would be quiet intolerable without it. Nothing contributed so much to keep my companions and myself clear of low fellowship and bad habits as the beneficence of the good Colonel.
>
> (p. 46)

> ...in this way, the windows were opened in the walls of my dungeon through which the light of knowledge streamed in. Every day's toil and even the long hours of night service were lightened by the books which I carried about with me and read in the intervals that could be snatched from duty. And the future was made bright by the thought that when Saturday came a new volume could be attained.
>
> (Carnegie, 1920, p. 46)

Carnegie goes on to write, "later, when fortune smiled upon me, one of my first duties was the erection of a monument to my benefactor" (p. 47). Today, across from the Carnegie Library of Pittsburgh, Allegheny Regional Branch, that monument to Colonel James Anderson stands. Below an elevated bust of the Colonel's watchful eyes there is another sculpture, one of a young man with chiseled muscles born out of hard work is sitting on an anvil reading a book. Below the "Reading Blacksmith," there is a plaque that reads:

> To Colonel James Anderson, founder of free libraries in Western Pennsylvania. He opened his library to working boys and on Saturday afternoons acted as a librarian, thus dedicating not only his books, but himself to the noble work. This monument is erected in grateful remembrance by Andrew Carnegie, one of the "working boys" to whom were thus opened the precious treasures of knowledge and imagination through which youth may ascend".[25]

Carnegie noted that it was from that early experience that he decided

> there was no use to which money could be applied so productive of good to boys and girls who have good within them and ability and ambition to develop it, as the founding of a public library in a community which is willing to support it as a municipal institution. . . . For if one boy in each library district, by having access to one of these libraries, is half as much benefited as I was by having access to Colonel Anderson's four hundred well-worn volumes, I shall consider they have not been established in vain.
>
> "As the twig is bent the tree's inclined." The treasures of the world which books contain were opened to me at the right moment.

(p. 47)

Andrew Carnegie attributed his business successes and generous benevolence to the learning and wisdom he gleaned from the teachers and mentors he found in books.

Notes

1 Judge David Wills to Abraham Lincoln, November 2, 1863. Manuscript Letter. [Invitation to speak at the consecration of a Civil War cemetery at Gettysburg, PA.] The Gettysburg Address. Robert Todd Lincoln Papers. Manuscript Division.
2 From Edward Everett papers, volume 120, letterbook, 23 October 1863-28 March 1884, p. 27. Retrieved from https://www.masshist.org/database/1780.

3 Everett was the leading intellectual and orator at the time of the Gettysburg Address. Everett served in the U.S. House of Representative and Senate, as governor of Massachusetts, U.S. ambassador to Great Britain, secretary of state, and President of Harvard. Everett's Gettysburg speech, as with his other speeches, were also steeped in classical literature and references.

4 An American computer scientist and Director of Research for Google Inc. The Powerpoint referenced can be found on his official webpage at https://norvig.com/Gettysburg/.

5 These words only make sense because of the historical reference found in a supertext, the Bible. The reference abounds with meaning and becomes a shortcut to rewording the sentence to something like

> The backstory is that the founders of such companies started out as one of many in field of equal and larger competitors when the odds for success were blatantly against them, except for their faith that gave them resolve and hope.

While both options convey the same message, the former solicits associations with the Bible and corresponding stories and messages.

6 National Aeronautics and Space Act of 1958, July, 29 1958 Pub. L. No. 85-568, 72 Stat. 426–438.

7 *Life Magazine*, October 21, 1957 Edition, p. 19.

8 Pangloss is a person who is optimistic regardless of the circumstances, a reference to a character by the same name in *Candide*, a satirical novel by Voltaire. Magoo is a reference to a lovable 1950s and 1960s television character who was portrayed as an older gentleman who had troubled seeing.

9 Information retrieved from the official online site for the John F. Kennedy Presidential Library and Museum.

10 There is discussion around which comes first, the story itself or the message of the story. The answer is both. Organizational vision creates real life stories and real-life stories inform the vision.

11 JFK even used language and cadence that connected his inaugural speech to the Gettysburg Address – "a century and three-quarters ago," "we dare not forget that we are heirs to that first revolution" and other references to resolve and service, including several easily remembered pithy statements and Biblical themes.

12 Winona is relatively unique in that is the home to several multi-million dollar international manufacturing companies, including Hal Leonard Publishing, Knitcraft Corporation, Peerless Chain, and The Watkins Company. The town of 27,000 people is also the home of Winona State University, Saint. Mary's University, and up to 1989, the College of Saint Teresa.

13 Henry Adams was the great grandson of John Quincy Adams and a prominent history professor at Harvard. *Mont St. Michel and Chartres* is a meditative reflection on history, culture, philosophy and worldview.

14 Mike saw business has a three legged stool – craftsmanship (i.e., product), selling, and back room (the management and logistical side of running a business).

15 Since 2007, the Minnesota Beethoven Festival has celebrated the music and legacy of Ludwig van Beethoven, in an unequaled environment of performance, discovery, and community, nestled in the quaint bluffs of southeast Minnesota.

16 The Minnesota Maritime Art Museum
    initial collections focused on traditional marine or maritime art, how-
    ever, through a collection on long-term loan, today the MMAM is home
    to a large variety of the greatest European and American masters. The
    MMAM is the public home to masterpieces by Turner, Monet, Renoir, Van
    Gogh, Cassatt, Gauguin, Picasso, Matisse, Kandinsky, O'Keeffe, Homer,
    Wyeth, and many more.

17 Perry (2014) reported that 88% of the Fortune 500 companies in 1955 were
    gone in 2014. *The Bureau of Labor Statistics documented* that since 1995 about half
    the businesses, regardless of the sector, survive after five years and less than
    30% after 15 years.

18 Bounded rationality is the principle that the human capacity for making con-
    sequential administrative decisions is bounded by cognitive limitations and
    time. First described by Herbert Simon in his studies on administrative behav-
    ior and decision making, bounded rationality recognizes that decision makers
    are not omniscient and omnipotent. As a result of incomplete information and
    uncertainty, decisions are bounded by the knowledge at hand at the time of the
    decision, refuting the myth that people can make fully rational decisions.

19 Bill Margaritis, Corporate Vice President, Global Communications and In-
    vestor Relations at the time of Forman's case study.

20 While content is king in storytelling, the queen is the delivery. Denning (2011)
    stated that

    everything is transformed in appearance. Small things make a big differ-
    ence. The look of the eye, the intonation of the voice, the way the body is
    held, the import of a subtle pause, the teller's response to the audience's
    response – all these aspects make a huge contribution to the meaning of a
    story for audiences.

                                                                    (pp. 11–12)

21 Personae is plural for persona and is word derived from Latin that originally
    meant theatre mask, reinforcing the concept of leader as performer developed
    by Erving Goffman (1959), *The Presentation of Self in Everyday Life* cited earlier.

22 Carnegie Corporation of New York official website.

23 Originally published in the North American Review (as "Wealth"), Vol. CXLVIII,
    June 1889.

24 Andrew initiated a $15 million pension fund for aged university professors
    (The Carnegie Endowment for the Advancement of Learning) noting that "of
    all the professions, that of teaching is probably the most unfairly yes, most
    meanly paid, though it should rank with the highest. Educated men, devot-
    ing their lives to teaching the young, receive mere pittances" (Carnegie, 1920,
    p. 268).

25 Andrew goes on to note that his acquaintance with theatre and classical music
    would cultivate his tastes, on par with his debt to books (Carnegie, 1920, p. 49).

References

Bates, S. (1997). Sputnik. *American Heritage, 48*(2). Retrieved from https://www.
americanheritage.com/sputnik

Bolman, L. & Deal, T. (2013). *Reframing organizations: Artistry, choice, and leadership.* San Francisco, CA: JosseyBass.

Boritt, G. (2008). *The Gettysburg Gospel: The Lincoln speech that nobody knows.* New York, NY: Simon & Schuster.

Carnegie, W. (1920). *Autobiography of Andrew Carnegie.* London, England: Constable & CO.

Carton, A. M. (2018). "I'm not mopping the floors, I'm putting a man on the moon": How NASA leaders enhanced the meaningfulness of work by changing the meaning of work. *Administrative Science Quarterly, 63*(2), 323–369. https://doi.org/10.1177/0001839217713748

Denning, S. (2007). *The secret language of leadership: How leaders inspire action through narrative.* San Francisco, CA: Jossey-Bass.

Denning, S. (2010). *The leader's guide to radical management.* San Francisco, CA: JosseyBass.

Denning, S. (2011). *The leader's guide to storytelling: Mastering the art and discipline of business narrative.* San Francisco, CA: JosseyBass.

Dolan, G. & Naidu, Y. (2013). *Hooked: How leaders connect, engage and inspire with storytelling.* Melbourne, VIC: John Wiley & Sons Australia.

Dreisbach, D. (2015). Biblical language and themes in Lincoln's Gettysburg Address. *Perspectives on Political Science, 44*(1), 34–39. doi: 10.1080/10457097.2014.955447

Elmore, A. E. (2009). *Lincoln's Gettysburg address: Echoes of the Bible and Book of Common Prayer.* Carbondale: Southern Illinois University Press.

Forman, J. (2013). *Storytelling in business: The authentic and fluent organization.* Palo Alto, CA: Stanford University Press.

Goffman, E. (1959). *The presentation of self in everyday life.* New York, NY: Anchor Books.

Guber, P. (2007, December). The Four Truths of the Storyteller. *Harvard Business Review.*

Hutchinson, K. (2018). *Leadership and small business: The power of stories.* Cham, Switzerland: Springer Nature.

Kierlin, R. (2015). *The power of Fastenal people.* Winona, MN: Fastenal Company.

Kierlin, R. (1993). *The unified theory of life.* Roseville, MN: The Dorsch Group.

Levine, A. (1982). *Managing NASA in the Apollo era.* Washington, DC: National Aeronautical Space Association. Retrieved from https://ntrs.nasa.gov/archive/nasa/casi.ntrs.nasa.gov/19830010280.pdf

Maitlis, S., & Christianson, M. (2014). Sensemaking in organizations: Taking stock and moving forward. *The Academy of Management Annals, 8*(1), 57–125.

McGinn, D. (2017). Leading, not managing, in crisis. *Harvard Business Review.* Retrieved from https://hbr.org/2017/11/leading-not-managing-in-crisis

Peatman, J. (2013). *The long shadow of Lincoln's Gettysburg Address.* Carbondale: Southern Illinois University Press.

Perry, M. (2014). Fortune 500 firms in 1995 vs. 2014. *Carpe Diem AEI.* Retrieved from http://www.aei.org/publication/fortune-500-firms-in-1955-vs-2014-89-are-gone-and-were-all-better-off-because-of-that-dynamic-creative-destruction/

Schein, E. H. (2010). *Organizational culture and leadership.* San Francisco, CA: JosseyBass.

Sidey, H. (1961, March 17). The president's voracious reading habits. *Life Magazine, 50*(11), 55–60.

Simon, H. (1964). On the concept of organizational goal. *Administrative Science Quarterly, 9*(1), 2–22. Retrieved from http://digitalcollections.library.cmu.edu/awweb/awarchive?type=file&item=33654

Weick, K. (1995). *Sensemaking in organizations.* Thousand Oaks, CA: Sage Publishing.

Wills, G. (2006). *Lincoln at Gettysburg: The words that remade America.* New York, NY: Simon & Schuster.

Index

Note: Page numbers followed by "n" denote endnotes.

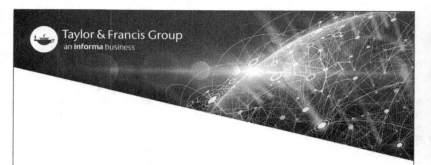

Printed in the United States
by Baker & Taylor Publisher Services